The Two Sandals

Intention, Attention and the Journey of Becoming Human

Etsko Schuitema

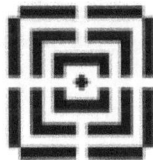

INTENT PUBLISHING

Title: The Two Sandals

Cover photo by Andries Nieuwoudt

Copyright © Etsko Schuitema 2016

Schuitema Associates cc trading as Intent Publishing

Postal address: PO Box 877, Walkerville, 1876

Physical Address:: 64 Cross Road, Walkers Fruit Farms, De Deur, 1884

+27 11 8670587

info@schuitemagroup.com Website: www.schuitemagroup.com

Print ISBN: 978-0-620-98880-3

About our logo: The square in the middle represents The One. From The One comes the two surrounding lines, the 'Outward' and the 'Inward'. The next four are the 'Sensory' and 'Meaning 'aspects of the 'Inward' and 'Outward', and the last eight the 'Celestial' and 'Terrestrial'
manifestations of the previous aspects

CONTENTS

Acknowledgement

While I have had many spiritual mentors and teachers over the years, no one has enabled my inner growth more than my beloved wife Tawheda. I owe her an unpayable debt of gratitude.

FORWARD ARMAND KRUGER

Living is like looking at life through a kaleidoscope, with an unknown hand continuously turning the hand piece and changing what there is to see. This book asks questions and offers answers that allow the reader to come up with a road map to understand and respond more appropriately to this kaleidoscope. The author of this book and his writing cannot be separated from each other. His life is evidence for the book. He has actively researched the themes in this book since 1984. He has presented these ideas in 26 countries, in some instances through the media of a translator. This is one piece of evidence of the trustworthiness and relevance of the information in this book.

Here are two things you will not find in this book:

1. Stories and myths about a universe on standby. The self-help wave at present is one of doing something and you will get: find the secret, visualize, be grateful, do three things to enhance your happiness and the universe will give you .... You will not find ways of inviting the universe to your party anywhere in this book. Gabrielle Oettingen refers to this as the cult of optimism.

2. Advice on 'all you have to do is ...' and you will have the life you want. Some of these do-to-get-myths are that happiness must be found; happiness will occur if you change your life's circumstances (more money,

different car, magnificent co-habitation partner), or even: you have it or you don't.

Current research is indicating that this cult of optimism may do more damage than good (http://www.cbsnews.com/news/positive-fantasies-hurt-real-world-success/).

THE TWO SANDALS

Against this tide comes a timeous and relevant book that maps out a gentle, but firm journey and gives another take on the kaleidoscope called life. You need two sandals to walk life. The one sandal is your intent. The other sandal is how and what you pay attention to. Living with appropriate intent is the result of an incremental growth process. This process of growth to maturity might be considered by some as a spiritual journey. It is very definitely a way of answering some serious questions about living and the meaning of life. If the answer is: 'benevolent intent in the form of unconditional giving', what might the question be?

The companion sandal is the attention that reflects your intent. The more the emphasis is on 'getting' rather than 'giving', the more your focus, actions and energy will be about getting things. Then, of course, you will be a ready sucker for the cult of optimism, or the 'all I have to do is ...'-thought viruses. As you progress on this incremental journey of becoming mature and acquire the wisdom of right living, you will find a shift in that you are seeking more ways to give than to get. Then you will be a member of a universal group of people living the right life with wisdom.

How will the reader know this is an appropriate and worthwhile journey? The evidence for this thinking is to be found in multiple contexts: successful work, effective teams, and high personal well-being. This book will create the awareness that will alert you to find the evidence for these ideas in many spaces of your current life. The activities in the book allow you to explore many contexts and to be pleasantly surprised at the answers you discover waiting for you.

Armand Kruger is a psychologist, specialist NLP and Neuro-Semantics trainer and business consultant.

PREFACE

The title of this book, The Two Sandals, is derived from the Sufi spiritual tradition, where the metaphor of two sandals is commonly used to describe progress on the path of spiritual maturation. However, the interpretation of what the two sandals denote is very often left up to the shaykh (teacher or spiritual guide) concerned.

To my mind, the two sandals represent what I believe are the two principal variables that are at issue on the path of inner unfoldment, namely intention and attention. Just as sandals protect the feet of the traveller and enable one to cover greater distances than if it had been undertaken barefoot, any path that does not give one tools in either of these realms will present the aspirant with a less than adequate tool kit. It will likely lead to an unnecessarily difficult and lengthy journey on the path of spiritual awakening.

This book is a development on my previous book Intent: Exploring the Core of Being Human. While much of the initial content (on intent) is similar, working with the material for two decades has led to a deepening of my understanding and a clearer articulation of the ideas. The latter end of the book explores the issue of attention.

THE MODELS

The Eight Attentions

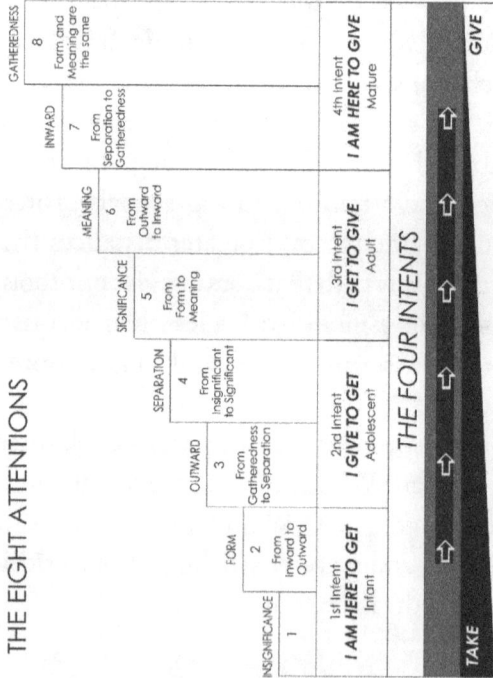

THE MODELS

The Eight Attentions

THE EIGHT ATTENTIONS

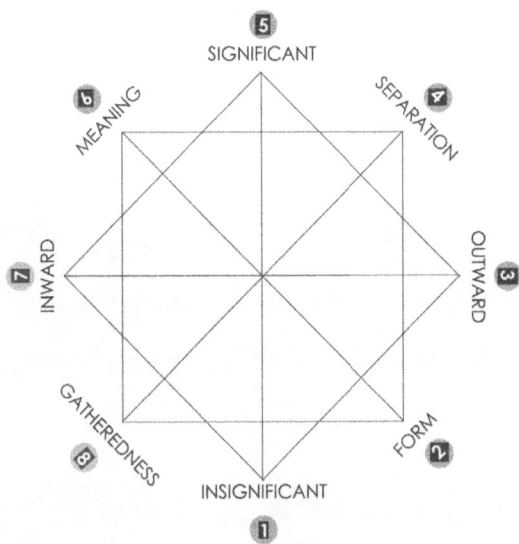

SIGNIFICANT

SEPARATION

MEANING

OUTWARD

INWARD

FORM

GATHEREDNESS

INSIGNIFICANT

THE MODELS

Transactional Correctness

TRANSACTIONAL CORRECTNESS			
BENEVOLENT INTENT		**MALEVOLENT INTENT**	
INWARD SELF SEER	OUTWARD OTHER SEEN	INWARD SELF SEER	OUTWARD OTHER SEEN
ESSENCE Awe	Signiicance	Terror	Arrogance
ATTRIBUTE Submission	Power	Rebellion	Control
PRIMARY ELEMENT Trust	Courage	Distrust	Cowardice
SECONDARY ELEMENT Gratitude	Generosity	Resentment	Selishness
ROOT *Seeing things as they are*	*Giving each situation it's due*	*Presumption*	*Expediency*

Chapter 1

ASPIRATION

I t is a cold February morning in Jersey (British Isles) in 2010. have a group of ten people n the room with me for the day. The subject we are exploring s the ssue of personal excellence.

This group is by no means a typical twenty-first century group of people. They are exclusively Caucasian, many of them native Jersey Islanders, with a single South African (other than me) in the room. They all work for a successful wealth management company. These are privileged people.

However, what makes them interesting is not that they are unique. It is that their views are so incredibly consistent with the views that I have solicited from people all over the world, from many different walks of life, on the issue of what it means to succeed.

I asked the group to reflect on the question 'what are the possible criteria for success?' and to produce a list of words. I then captured what was said in a single list that is reflected in the table on the next page.

The first thing that became apparent to me is that I had seen this kind of content produced before, and not only in response to the question 'what are the possible criteria of success?' but to any number of questions one could ask in order to explore the issue of what is important to someone.

Questions like:
- Why do you go to work?
- What do you aspire to?
- What do you worry about?
- What motivates you?
- What does achievement look like to you?

The reason for such consistency in the responses is because all these questions are different ways of getting to the same thing: They are all concerned with exploring the issue of intent – of why people do things.

What are the Possible Criteria for Success?

Happiness, Contentment, Wealth, Power, Life-balance, Family, Respect, Achievement, Success, Personal Goals, Intellect, Fame, Health, Status, Acceptance, Responsibility, Love, Recognition, Popularity, Application, Knowing your Weaknesses, Acceptance of Others, Learning, Drive, Ambition, Sacrifice, Achieving Potential.

It suggests then that regardless of how one constructs an investigation into what motivates people, when you get down to what their real intent is, one gets a very similar set of answers. What is also apparent is that the answers to these questions can be grouped into five quite distinct categories.

In the first instance the answers reflect a concern for security. For example, the Jersey group indicated variables such as (a safe) personal environment, financial reward, wealth and health. Other questions and other groups would reflect a similar concern for security, with people noting things like stability, earning a living, providing for their family and providing for their retirement.

The second theme in this information is concerned with fulfilment or contentment. The Jersey group indicated things such as planning, life balance, happiness, contentment. Further to this, people might list variables like beauty, creativity or spirituality.

The third theme, which is concerned with power or significance from other people, manifested in the Jersey group with attributes such as recognition, power, respect, achievement, success, fame, status, popularity, drive and ambition being listed.

Some of the attributes listed here caused some debate among the group as to which category it should fall in. For example, it was agreed that if what was meant by achievement was a sense of personal growth, it would more naturally fall in the fulfilment category. However, if the same word brought a competitive sense to mind for a person, then it really referred to the issue of coming first, or being above other people, and would resonate with the issue of power.

As an aside, this Jersey group seemed quite brazen and shameless in confessing to the importance that power held for them. Most groups I deal with are much more politically correct in this regard and may not even indicate anything relating to power at all.

Themes of Criteria for Success	
Personal environment, Financial reward, Wealth, Health.	SECURITY
Planning, Life-balance, Happiness, Contentment.	FULFILMENT
Recognition, Power, Respect, Achieve-ment, Success, Fame, Status, Popularity, Drive, Ambition.	POWER
Family, Sacrifice, Love, Acceptance, Responsibility, Accep-tance of Others.	HARMONY
Learning, Intellect, Personal Application, Personal Goals, Know-ing your Weaknesses, Achieving Potential.	GROWTH

Be that as it may, the issue of power over others as a variable is always present – albeit latently. It can be surfaced by asking a question such as 'All things such as benefits and pay being equal, would people move from one job to another if the next job was more senior?' With most groups, one would get a reasonably unanimous positive answer to this question. Power is, without a doubt, a core aspect of human intent.

The fourth theme, which is harmony, seems somewhat at odds with the previous one. The issue of power really has a competitive feel to it, whereas some of the ideas raised by the

> ❛We do not often consider our inward space, the subjective, as a legitimate and worthy realm of work. It is as if we consider the objective world as the only place worthy of serious attention.❜

Jersey islanders had a far more co-operative sense to them, such as family, sacrifice, love, responsibility and acceptance of others. Again, with some of these ideas, one needs to explore the intent that sits behind them to establish which category they fit into. An idea like 'responsibility' may also be seen to be concerned with the security theme in the sense of providing for one's family.

The final theme, growth, is difficult to distinguish from the fulfillment theme, and is arguably best seen as a subset of it. For the Jersey group, this included issues like learning, intellect, personal application, personal goals, knowing your weaknesses and achieving potential. Again, some of these items need to be interrogated a bit further to establish the real motive. 'Personal goals' and 'achieving potential' can be seen to be consistent with the power theme if these goals are competitive in character and the potential is concerned with winning or coming first.

Elsewhere I have seen the following terms that would be consistent with this growth theme: challenge, exploration, developing skills, refinement, capability, understanding, insight and so on.

It appears that one could reduce our intent to four, maybe five themes: Security, fulfillment, power, harmony and growth, with growth possibly being seen as a subset of the fulfillment theme. This is why people do things; it is what they aspire to and commit endeavor and effort toward.

What is very important about this endeavor is where it is conducted and to what purpose. We mostly conduct it in the objective world with the intent to produce an outcome in the world. In fact, when we consider the words 'work' or 'aspiration' or 'endeavor', they have a bias to outward and objective activity. We do not often consider our inward space, the subjective, as a legitimate and worthy realm of work. It is as if we consider the objective world as the only place worthy of serious attention; and that the realm of the inward is the realm of the subjective and illusory.

The Window of Perception

If we consider how we actually experience things, this assumption does not reflect our reality. At the limit of my peripheral vision, there is a boundary that acts like a window frame. Everything I perceive presents itself within that frame. One could refer to that frame as the window of perception. What is inside that frame is the objective world, that which I perceive. Most of the work that people do that aims at producing happiness is done in that objective, perceived world. The place that I perceive from, is behind this window.

That place is the realm of my thoughts, dreams, ideals and intentions. The key contention in this chapter is that the elements of security, fulfilment, power, harmony and growth are attributes of how one's intent operates. The variable of intent is to be found on the inside, behind the window of perception. So it suggests that most of us commit the endeavour and work aimed at achieving security, fulfillment, power, harmony and growth in the wrong place.

These things are not a result of work done in the outward; they are the product of work done in the inward, in the realm of intent. To think that we are going to achieve what we aspire to by committing endeavour to the outward is therefore like me scratching my backside to get at an itch on my head.

How Intent Works

To commence this exploration we need to consider how intent operates. In order to understand the fundamental architecture of intent, we need to recognise that it is virtually impossible to explore the issue without recognising the foundation that intent stands on, namely the distinction between the self and the other.

All our experience assumes a fundamental binary opposite, the distinction between the self and the other.

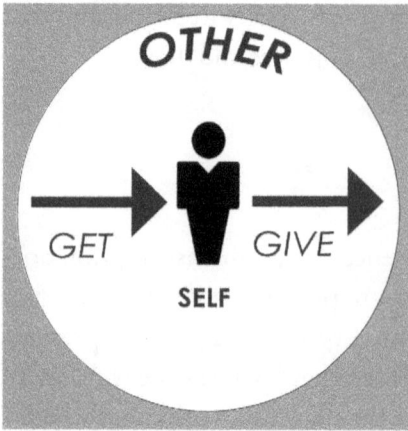

The other presents itself as that which encapsulates the self. If I point at other than myself, I can turn a full circle and still be pointing at other than myself. The other surrounds the self. The experience of the self is presented in such a way as to suggest that the other stretches in every direction, in a bubble or sphere, away from the self. In this sense, the self is in the middle of it all; it is the-epicenter of being.

There are also two fundamental processes at work in the engagement between the self and the other. There is that which is concerned with what the self gets. In other words, that which moves from the other to the self. And that which the self gives, that which moves from the self to the other. When one examines intent, it becomes apparent that one can either hook one's intent onto what one wants to get from the other or what one gives to the other. Which one of these two we hook our intent to, has dramatic consequences for what we aspire to.

The Effect of Intent on Security

The first thing that becomes apparent regarding the difference between what one gets and what one gives is that what one gets rests in the power of the other. Whereas what one gives, lies in the power of the self. This holds significant implications for security.

If I base my security on what I get from the world – because the world rarely gives what I want at that particular point in time – I will always be insecure. This is because the universe is too big and complex to be able to deliver a set of conditions that are going to suit me right now.

On the other hand, I always have control over the quality of what I am contributing at any given point in time, which suggests that if I base my security on what I am contributing, I will always be secure. This means that to think that there is any relationship between what I get or what I own and how secure I am, is naïve. We have all known people who are very secure despite not owning much. The idea that there is a bank account which is big enough to scratch the itch called insecurity does not recognise that this itch does not get scratched by what comes from the other to the self, but what leaves the self for the other.

> ❝ What one gets rests in the power of the other, ... whereas what one gives, lies in the power of the self. This holds significant implications for security. ❞

When one examines what you are really assuming when you base your security on things in the world, then it becomes apparent that you think those things will stand between you and disaster. That which makes you secure protects you, it interposes itself between you and catastrophe. A very good example of this is ownership of a house. In the community that I come from, the assumption is that once you have paid off the bankers

‘ My possessions do not serve me, I serve them. My possessions do not look after me, I look after them. In fact, one can make a very firm argument that the more things I own, the less secure I am. ’

and have control over the title deeds of your property, you are secure. What is implied in this sense of security is that your house will protect you. It will stand between you and disaster.

What this does not recognise is that there is no asset that will stand between you and disaster. In fact, the very idea is ludicrous. Assume I am the subject of a vicious assault today, and I arrive at home bleeding profusely from several terrible wounds to the head. I very much doubt that as I drag my bloodied body up the garden path, my house will react in outrage. I can't see it saying, 'Etsko! Who hit you? Where is he?! Let me at him!'

In fact, my house does not care in the least that someone assaulted me today. It will respond today in much the same way as it had yesterday, before I was attacked. It is supremely fickle, in fact. If my assailant had killed me in this attack and had the gall to sleep in my bed tonight, my house would not be in the least concerned. It would not say to him 'Hey? Who are you? What have you done with Etsko?' On the other hand, if I walk up the garden path this afternoon and see that the neighbourhood hooligans had sprayed a red X on my front door, I would be incensed. I would certainly want to find out who did this, and I would seek retribution. So the question is, am I there to look after my house or is my house there to look after me? Clearly, I look after my house.

Nothing that I own recognises a custodial responsibility toward me. However, I certainly have a custodial charge with regard to what I own.

That this is true is borne out by my immense displeasure when something happens to my stuff. My possessions do not serve me, I serve them. My possessions do not look after me, I look after them. In fact, one can make a very firm argument that the more things I own, the less secure I am.

When I base my security on what I get or own, I am insecure. When I base my security on what I contribute or give, I am secure. Security is therefore not a product of what I get or own, it is a product of the degree to which I base my intent on giving or serving.

> ❝ When I base my security on what I get or own, I am insecure. When I base my security on what I contribute or give, I am secure. ❞

The Effect of Intent on Fulfilment

The same arguments which demonstrate that security is a product of the intent to give, also demonstrate that fulfilment is the product of the intent to give. The world rarely gives me exactly what I want at any given point in time. If I base my happiness on what I am getting from the world, I will be discontented. If I base my fulfilment and happiness on what I am contributing, I am basing it on something I always have control over. I will always be contented. Anyone who has felt the deep sense of contentment flowing from doing a job well, will know that this is true.

This is why it is curious that as a species, we behave like lemmings in the pursuit of the American dream. It is as if we have all committed to the North American definition of the good life as the standard for fulfilment. If these people were so immensely happy, why is it that their societies are so violent, their populations so drugged up and their people so obese?

> ❛ If I want something from someone else, that person's ability to withhold what I want gives them power over me. ❜

Clearly, this Elysium Americana, the place of perfect happiness, is not what it purports to be. To own is not to be happy. The neediness that drives this material definition of the good life overlooks the wisdom of austerity, of deliberately making do with little and taking pleasure in making do with little. Luggage is a beautiful metaphor for this. The more bags there are to drag about, the more attention needs to be given to your stuff. The more the bags, the less attention there is for the place you are in, to explore the new, to learn, to be exposed. The more the bags, the slower the journey.

The more the bags, the more there is to hold on to, to defend from the thugs. The more bags, the more you are occupied by what you have brought with you. As they say, "You have baggage and to have baggage is to have issues."

The Effect of Intent on Power

If I want something from someone else, that person's ability to withhold what I want gives them power over me. On the other hand, if I want to give someone something, then they have no power over me.

If, for example, you are the proud owner of a very good watch and I want the watch, then you are able to withhold the watch. You have power over me. If I shift my intention from the watch that I want from you to how I can be helpful to you, you cannot withhold anything. You no longer have power over me.

All our weakness is based on the intent to get and all our power is based on the intent to give. This is why suicide bombers have such a disproportionate effect compared with their numbers. They are willing to give or lose everything, unconditionally. This logic does not only hold true for dramatic situations such as suicide bombings; every transaction has the same logic. In any transaction, the party that can lose the transaction first sets the price. The person who cannot lose the transaction is clearly still negotiable. They do not define the transaction, but the transaction defines them. You have power over what you are able to give or lose; and you are in the power of what you cannot lose.

There is a quaint Sufi story that demonstrates this theme:

A party of pirates were shipwrecked in a storm, but managed to scramble onto a boat. One of the pirates managed to rescue a bag of gold coins before he leapt into the water.

He struggled desperately to get to the boat, but the treasure was very heavy and made it virtually impossible for him to reach the boat. His shipmates shouted at him to let go of the bag because it was dragging him under.

His valiant struggle continued for a few more minutes but, soon enough, the treasure dragged him down, and he disappeared beneath the waves. The drama deeply affected the survivors in the boat, who remained sunk in a morose silence for a couple of hours.

Finally, one of the party sighed heavily and commented 'Poor bugger, he had to have his gold'. A second pirate snorted in derision: 'Don't be ridiculous,' he said. 'He did not have his gold. His gold had him.'

If you cannot lose something, you don't have it; it has you. We have power over what we can give or lose, but are also in the power of what we want to get.

The Effect of Intent on Harmony

Remember: if I want something from someone else, that person's ability to withhold what I want gives them power over me. They are strong and I am weak. That also implies that they are potentially dangerous to me because I have given them the power to manipulate me.

> *Any conflict you have with someone else says much more about you than about the person you have the dispute with. This is particularly true when the conflict makes you rancorous. You can only be upset with someone because they are not rising to your expectations.*

However, because I want something from them, I am also dangerous to them. If someone wants to get something out of you, you experience them as hostile to your interests. You experience them as dangerous to you. So if you want something from someone else, that person is dangerous to you, and simultaneously you are dangerous to them. And when two people are fundamentally dangerous to each other, the only possible outcome is conflict.

On the other hand, if I want to give someone something, they cannot withhold anything from me, which means I am safe from that person because they cannot manipulate me. Not only am I safe from them, but they are safe from me, precisely because I want to give them something rather than to get something out of them. I am safe from them and they are safe from me. We therefore have harmony.

This suggests that any conflict you have with someone else says much more about you than about the person you have the dispute with. And this is particularly true when the conflict makes you rancorous. You can only be upset with someone because they are not rising to your expectations.

The degree to which your intent with the other is unconditional is the degree to which you do not have expectations that may not be met. This does not mean that you would not confront a person, but your confrontation would be in a spirit of 'take it or leave it', and will not leave you rancorous.

It will be a confrontation in the interest of the person rather than to get something out of that person. One of the implications of this is that the difference between conflict and harmony is not so much a difference in behaviour, but a difference in intent. In my own life the experience I had that most exemplified this was concerned with a man who I shall refer to as Loutjie Steyn. I met him in the mid nineteen eighties. He was a mine overseer on a gold mine I did consulting work for, as a representative of the Chamber of Mines Research Organisation.

> 'The difference between conlict and harmony is not so much a difference in behaviour, but a difference in intent.'

At the time, I was a youth in my twenties and Loutjie Steyn was a grizzled mining man in his mid-forties. He was a very tall man, powerfully built with a black belt in karate. He also had the most disturbing reputation for assaulting people underground. His reputation eventually got known in the hallowed halls of the company's head office, which reacted in horror. Bear in mind that this was the mid nineteen eighties, and trade unions were sweeping through the industry like an avenging tide. As a result, the head office of the company sent an instruction to the mine that Loutjie Steyn should be redeployed.

Management on the mine removed Loutjie Steyn from his mining job, giving him a desk-bound planning job instead. It was a specialist role where he had nobody reporting to him, so the assumption was that he would keep his hands off people. However, to the dismay of all the senior people concerned, his entire team of several hundred men went on strike. They wanted their mine overseer back.

After a standoff of some days, management finally relented and put Loutjie Steyn back in his job.

> **❛** We do not only produce what it feels like to be in our own skins, we also produce the world we are in. **❜**

What remained, however, was great confusion. It was inexplicable to senior management that employees would strike support of a leader who had a reputation for assaulting them.

The confusion was cleared up some months later when there was a serious fall of ground in Loutjie Steyn's section. He was the last man out of the section. He had gone in, time and again, to rescue people until he had accounted for all of them. This explained why his men were loyal to him, why they were in a state of harmony with him, despite the fact that he was harsh with them. They knew he had their backs, that he was sincere with them. They knew he was there for them and not to get something out of them.

When he was faced with the choice between doing what was expedient to him or putting his interests on the line for his people, he acted in their interests. When he was faced with the choice between what was the right thing to do and what was in his immediate self-interest, he did what was right. He was demonstrably there to give.

A particularly significant implication of this insight is that we do not only produce what it feels like to be in our own skins, we also produce the world we are in.

Assume I have thirty engagements with other people in the course of a day. If, in my very first engagement, my intent is to take, it would produce a fundamentally conflicted engagement. If I then repeat that engagement thirty times over, my perception of the world that I inhabit would be that it is a very hostile place. They are all out to get me.

Conversely, if I deliberately build each one of my engagements on the basis of how I can be helpful, then the product of each one of those engagements will be harmony. My reflection on the world before I drift off to sleep that night will be that it is a very friendly place, populated with allies.

The Effect of Intent on Growth

We have established that if the self engages the other with the intent to get something from the other, the other's ability to withhold what the self wants gives the other power over the self. Simply put, when you engage the other with the intent to take, the other defines the self and the self gets stuck. The self stagnates. On the other hand, when the self deals with the other on the basis of the intent to contribute,

the other loses its power over the self. The self slips out from under the other's ability to control the self, and therefore the self grows and transcends the situation. All growth means that you have become bigger than yourself. You have gone beyond yourself; you have transcended yourself. The boundaries that confined you before are no longer operative. More than anything else our boundaries are constituted by expectations and our conditional motive. Every time we act on the basis of the best interest of the other, we transcend our own conditioning. We grow.

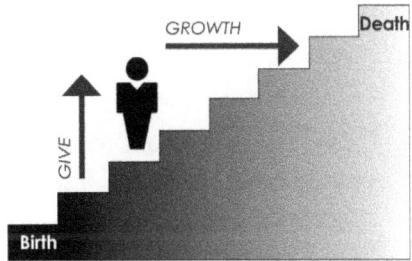

> ' All growth means that you have become bigger than yourself. You have gone beyond yourself; you have transcended yourself. The boundaries that confined you before are no longer operative. '

Aspiration as the Product of Intent

At the beginning of this chapter I sought to demonstrate that what we aspire to in our lives can be reduced to four or possibly five categories, namely security, fulfilment, power, harmony and growth, with the understanding that we can also see growth as a subset of the category of fulfillment.

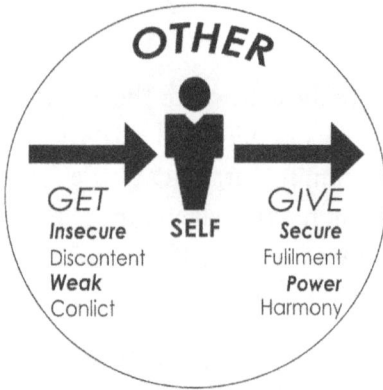

OTHER

GET — GIVE

Insecure SELF **Secure**

Discontent Fulilment

Weak **Power**

Conlict Harmony

❝ If we construct our intent on the basis of what we want to get, we will feel insecure, discontented, weak and in conlict with the world around us. When we construct our intent on what we can contribute, we produce an experience of security, fulilment, power and harmony. ❞

Our key contention here is that these things are not an attribute of any work done in the world, *in* the window of perception. These things are attributes of things that happen in the self, *behind* the window of perception. It means that all the work we do which is aimed at achieving these things is futile in so far as it is done in the world. This treasure is not to be found in the light of the outer world; it is to be found in the veiled shadow of the inner world where our intent operates.

We manufacture what it feels like to be in our own skins. If we construct our intent on the basis of what we want to get, we will feel insecure, discontented, weak and in conflict with the world around us. When we construct our intent on the basis of what we can contribute, we produce an experience of security, fulfilment, power and harmony.

This is immensely significant. I suspect that most people in our current culture have a somewhat tortured experience of being in their own skin. I would not be surprised that when Jane Doe goes to bed at night the register of her internal dialogue and her description of the day is one of insecurity, discontentment, weakness and conflict. Furthermore, if you ask her why she feels like that she will blame everybody else. The fault will be with the spouse, the kids, the boss, the colleagues, the subordinates, the neighbours or the government. The fault will lie with someone else.

Little does she recognise that this miserable experience of being in her own skin is her own product. She can have unconditional access to security, fulfilment, power and harmony, but she will have to pay the price. The price being, to shift her intent in her engagement with the world from what she wants to get, to what she wants to give.

This reminds me of a frequently repeated story that beautifully makes the point. It concerns the incomparable Mullah Nasrudin and has a number of variations to the theme, one of which is the following:

Mullah Nasrudin was an Imam (Muslim prayer leader or teacher) in a tiny village in Anatolia. One winter's morning he was seen frantically pacing up and down in front of his house peering at the ground. He became more and more distraught until he was shouting 'Oh God, it's gone. I've lost it. It's gone. It's gone, oh no, oh no!'

'What's gone, Mullah?' Ali, the village baker enquired sympathetically.

'My key, it's gone! I've lost the key to my house!

Oh what am I going to do?'

'Don't worry, sir,' Aisha, Ali's wife, crooned sympathetically, 'we will all help you to find it.'

Before long, the entire village were scraping their slippers through the snow, peering at the ground as they wandered to and fro, yet no one could find the key. After what seemed like a very long time (for it was very cold) Ali asked the Mullah:

'So Mullah, where exactly did you lose your key?' The Mullah pointed emphatically at his house.

'In the house,' he said.

'So why are we looking here?' Ali wanted to know, incredulously.

'Idiot!' barked the Mullah, 'There is a light here, I can see here! It's dark in the house!'

Chapter 2

MATURATION

T he shift from the intent to take to the intent to give is consistent with the process of maturation. If one considers maturation as a process, it implies that one can view it as an incremental progression from a beginning – birth – o he end, death.

Both moments – birth and death – have an unconditional character. At birth whatever the infant is going to get, it will still get, precisely because it has had nothing yet. The infant is therefore here to get everything. What that everything is, at that point, is irrelevant. The infant may only have two weeks of life ahead of it.

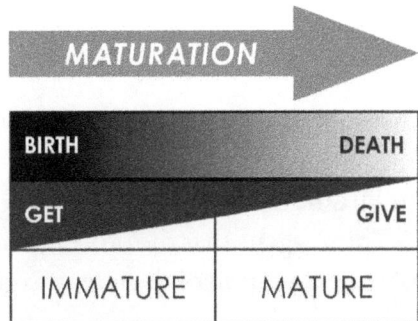

However, in the first moment, those two weeks are owed to the infant in their entirety. Everything he is to get he will still get. He is therefore here to get in the most unconditional sense of the word.

You can't take anything with you when you die, which means at death one gets nothing; you rather give everything, unconditionally. The logical challenge to this, however, is to say that when I die, I don't give anything; everything gets taken away from me.

This therefore creates another question, which is what is the difference between giving everything and having everything taken from you? Let us assume that Vusi has R1000 stolen from him, while Dianne gives R1000 to a neighbour who can't pay her mortgage and is in danger of losing her home. Is there a difference between what happened to Vusi and Dianne?

From one point of view, there is no difference. In both of their cases they no longer have the R1000 that they had before. So the difference does not lie in the R1000 – rather in the object.

> **❝** The process of maturation is by definition the process of the maturation of the intent to give unconditionally. **❞**

However, if we examine what lies in the subject of Vusi and Dianne, there is a massive difference. Vusi did not intend to give the R1000, which means that he experienced it as having been taken from him. Dianne's experience, on the other hand, was that she gave the R1000 because she had intended to do so.

The difference between giving something and having it taken from you does not lie in the objective event; it lies in the intent of the person who is going through the experience.

If one views the loss of the R1000 as one would death – as something which is inevitable – the question to ask is which of their experiences of the loss of the R1000 can one describe as the successful experience? Clearly, it has to be Dianne's.

This suggests that the process of maturation is by definition the process of the maturation of the intent to give unconditionally.

Generosity and Courage

The intent to give unconditionally can, however, be misunderstood. It is not about always being pliant or sweet and is most certainly not about being a pushover. In fact, giving is not about being nice, it is about being appropriate. Sometimes being appropriate is nice, and sometimes it is not.

For example, assume Ayesha is at home one day and hears a knock on her door. She opens the door to see a sniffling eight-year-old who looks like he has not eaten in a week. 'So sorry to disturb you, ma'am, but I am very hungry. I can't remember when last I ate something. Could you please spare me a slice of bread? Please?' the child implores with a forlorn look in his eyes. If we assume that Ayesha was properly raised, then clearly the appropriate thing to do here is to give the child food.

On the other hand, let's assume that Robert, a strong and athletic young man, goes for a jog in the park and comes across a drama where a little old lady is being assaulted by a thug attempting to take her handbag. The thug and the lady are about the same size, and she is resisting him.

She does not want to give him the bag. If Robert has been like a knight and slap the thug about in an effort to rescue the old lady. That is what giving will mean in this case. While it is self-evident that Ayesha and Robert are both giving, there seems to be a contradiction if you examine these two engagements from a purely behavioural point of view: When Ayesha is giving, her behaviour is kindness personified, whereas when Robert is giving, his behaviour is brutal. This suggests that giving is not always about being nice, it is about being appropriate; and appropriate is not always nice.

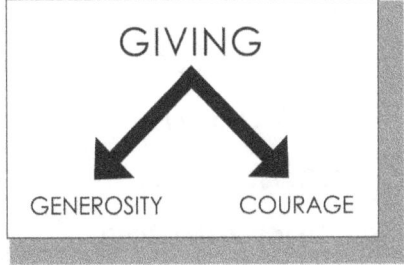

```
        GIVING

         /\
        /  \
       ↙    ↘
GENEROSITY   COURAGE
```

When we examine Ayesha's behaviour, it becomes clear that she was being generous.

> **❛ Giving is about being appropriate; it is about consistently acting with the courage or generosity that is operative or necessary in a situation. ❜**

Generosity is the appropriate word to describe someone who can give things easily and freely.

When we examine Robert's behaviour, it is clear that he was being courageous. Of the two, it is apparent that Robert is giving the most. Where Ayesha is putting things associated with herself on the line, Robert is putting himself on the line. We can therefore describe generosity as rising above one's fear of loss of things associated with the self, and courage as rising above the fear of loss of self.

If we argue that giving is about being appropriate – that it is about consistently acting with the courage or generosity that is operative or necessary in a situation – then it implies that you are getting your logic wrong when you act in a so-called generous way when you should be courageous, and in a so-called courageous way when you should be generous.

If, for example, Ayesha answers the knock at the door and when faced with the hungry child, she slaps him instead of giving him food, we would be understandably upset. We would be astonished if she argued that she was being courageous. We would not think her behaviour courageous at all. We would think she was selfish.

Similarly, if Robert came across the mugging incident and dealt with it by taking the bag out of the old woman's hands and giving it to the thug, we would also be non-plussed. Our discomfort would turn to outrage if he then quipped that he was being generous.

We can therefore say that if we act in a so-called courageous way when a situation requires generosity, we are not giving – we are taking. That taking is called selfish- ness. And if we act in a so- called generous way when a situation requires courage, we are also not giving – we are taking. That taking is called cowardice.

We started this chapter by observing that the process of maturation is consistent with the process of the maturation of the intent to give unconditionally. We also found that giving is not about being nice, it is about being appropriate. And that appropriateness presents itself in two categories, namely generosity and courage. It should, therefore, follow that as people mature, they become more generous and courageous.

To further a better understanding of how appropriate or inappropriate

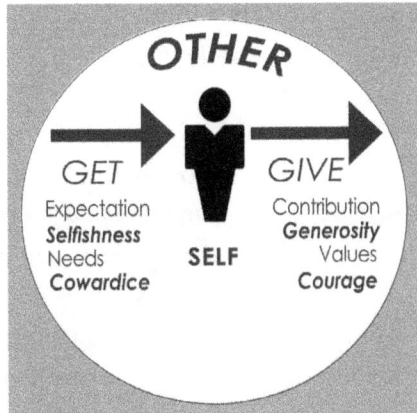

❛ If we act in a so-called courageous way when a situation requires generosity, we are not giving – we are taking. That taking is called selfishness. And if we act in a so-called generous way when a situation requires courage, we are also not giving – we are taking. That taking is called cowardice. **❜**

giving changes during the maturation process of the individual, it is useful to draw up a list, as I do with my groups, of the binary opposites of maturity and immaturity of actions and attitudes within these two categories or themes – the generous and the courageous.

The first grouping, in the generous category, shares a common theme of kindness. It is as if the mature side of the list of opposites indicates a generous approachability of spirit, while people experience immature people as dealing with whatever faces them from the point of view of expectation. So when an immature person deals with the other, his or her concern is what the other can do for them, rather than the other way around. Conversely, mature people seem more concerned with the contribution they should be making – what the other requires of them – rather than what they require from the other.

The second set of themes – the courageous category – seems to speak to demands made on people in certain situations. As one matures, you increasingly focus your intent on doing what is right, even though you fully understand that it may not always be expedient; that it may require you to act for reasons that are greater than your self-interest. I have chosen to refer to these larger reasons as values.

Mature individuals are values-driven; they are willing to take a bullet for something. On the opposite, immature side, we find needs-driven people – ones who are fundamentally expedient in their behaviour. They do what works for them and never stick their necks out for anything. Values-driven people are therefore courageous, whereas needs-driven people are cowardly.

Themes of the Generous Category

The accompanying table contains a typical set of themes that I would include in the list of the generous category.

One behaviour that, for me, encapsulates all of these opposites is the distinction between listening and not listening. We have all had an experience where we tried to explain something to someone else and they had even finished speaking. When this happens, it becomes apparent that there are two agendas in the room, and that the other person is really only giving attention to their own agenda.

For them to listen to you, they have to suspend their own agenda temporarily. The degree to which they do that completely is the degree to which you experience them as actually listening to you. This implies that to listen to someone properly requires one to suspend one's agenda for theirs. It indicates that listening is a moral skill, because it requires giving. One can describe this giving as the ability to suspend your own agenda for the agenda of the other in the situation you are in.

IMMATURE	MATURE
Taking	Giving
Selfish	Altruistic
Expectation	Contribution
Does not listen	Listens
Unapproachable	Approachable
Subjective	Objective
Closed mind	Free-thinking
Presumptuous	Not presumptuous
Irrational	Rational
Emotional	Relective
Opinionated	Not opinionated
Volatile	Calm
Intolerant	Tolerant
Disrespectful	Respectful
Discourteous	Courteous
Thoughtless	Considerate
Arrogant	Humble
Pretentious	Unassuming
Demeaning	Afirming
Competitive	Co-operative
Destructive	Constructive
Conlict	Harmony

This is why people frequently describe immature people as unapproachable and mature people as approachable.

Assume I am marching down the corridor in pursuit of my agenda, and someone approaches me to ask me something. Should I be an approachable person, I will obviously stop and give the person who approaches me my attention. In order to do that, I will have to forgo my agenda temporarily in order to give attention to theirs.

> ❛The impatience of needing to have one's own way, or the last word, is quintessentially immature. It is about not being able to suspend one's own agenda, or delay gratiication. It is about having what I want, now. ❜

One of the consequences of not being able to suspend one's own agenda is that other people experience one as subjective. Because my agenda sits in my subject when I only give attention to my own agenda, other people are likely to find me subjective. I should therefore, not be surprised if they consider me to have a closed mind, to be opinionated, irrational and emotional. These are all attributes people associate with immaturity.

Because someone else's agenda sits in my object when I suspend my agenda for theirs, they are likely to find me objective, as having an open, free-thinking mind. They will probably also consider me to be rational, reflective and reasonable. It stands to reason that they will judge me to be an un-opinionated and un-presumptuous person. People consider such a person mature.

The dismissiveness that comes with not being willing or able to listen to others and suspend one's own agenda creates conditions where other people experience us as disrespectful and arrogant. It produces intolerance and impatience, where other people experience us as demeaning of others and, in time, destructive. This impatience of needing to have one's own way, or the last word, is what is quintessentially immature. It is about not being able to suspend one's own agenda, or delay gratification. It is about having what I want, now. Joachim de Posada has built a successful speaking and writing career on just this theme – not eating the marshmallow right now.

Because mature people are able to suspend their agenda for the agenda of the other, they are experienced as fundamentally affirming of the other. They are respectful, considerate, unassuming and humble. Because this is the case, other people experience them as constructive and harmonious in their engagements.

Themes of the Courageous Category

The ability to delay gratification that comes with maturity also lies at the root of the courageous themes. Immature people are needs-driven in their behaviour, whereas mature people are values-driven.

IMMATURE	MATURE
Needs	Values
Can't delay gratification	Delays gratification
Impatient	Patient
Impulsive	Restrained
Short term	Long term
Irresponsible	Responsible
Expedient	Appropriate
Inconsistent	Consistent
Unfair	Fair
Dishonest	Honest
Malicious	Benevolent
Untrustworthy	Trustworthy
Rights	Duties

Assume, for example, you are on a long car journey with a three-year-old and a thirty-year-old in the back of the car. Twenty kilometers before your destination the three-year-old suddenly announces, with a hint of desperation in his voice: 'I have to pee!' The appropriate thing to do is probably to stop, particularly if you want to avoid an unpleasant clean up. If, on the other hand, the thirty-year-old happened to say the same thing, you would most likely ask him to hold on a bit because you are almost at your destination. The assumption that you are working with here, is that the thirty-year-old probably knows it is inappropriate to pee in his friend's car.

> **'**You are only really considered to be true to a value if you remain true to that value when it is not in your interest to do so. **'**

He is therefore able to suspend his need in the interest of doing what is appropriate in the situation.

It is really this ability to act for a reason that is different from and bigger than what you want to get for yourself, that sits at the heart of all values-driven behaviour. If one considers any given value, for example, honesty, then it is true that one is only considered honest when you stay honest even when it is not in your interest to do so. If one asks people to define honesty, most of the definitions that they offer, relate to truthfulness. Any definition of honesty that does not refer to truthfulness will not make sense.

Say, for instance, we ask Aud where he lives, and he tells us honestly that he lives in Bangkok, we have not demonstrated that he is an honest man, even though he spoke the truth about living in Bangkok. However, if we ask him about something that could potentially harm his own interest, and he still speaks the truth, then we could safely assume that he is an honest man.

This means that you are only really considered to be true to the value (honesty, in this case) if you remain true to that value when it is not in your interest to do so. This is why the current use of the word 'value' to mean 'that which is important to one', is not helpful. My needs may be important to me, but they are not values. It is very important to a paedophile to do sexually motivated things to minors. However, it would sound really strange to describe that need as a value. Just because something is important to you does not make it a value.

I believe it is important to keep the word 'value' consistent with the idea of virtue. It refers to an order of reality that is bigger than one's self-interest, and against which one will place their self-interest second. Values help you to understand the right thing to do in a situation, and provide you with a reason to do what is right, particularly in situations where it is not going to suit you to do so.

When one looks at the issue of being values-driven from this point of view, it becomes apparent that being values-driven requires courage.

When we defined the rule for giving as being associated with the generous category, we indicated that it was about demonstrably suspending your own agenda for the agenda of the other in the situation that you were in. Being values- driven, however, puts the heat on that definition, because it is concerned with suspending your own agenda for what is right – and this may require courage, because what is right may not be consistent with the other person's agenda.

> 'Values help you to understand the right thing to do in a situation, and provide you with a reason to do what is right, particularly in situations where it is not going to suit you to do so. '

Honesty really reflects this issue. If I honestly give another person feedback that they do not want to hear, their explicit agenda in the situation will be for me to keep quiet. So if I act generously by suspending my agenda for theirs, I will not be honest with them. I have to be courageous and speak up, even if I upset them and they consequently think of me as a monster. Yet another element which demonstrates that being values-driven requires courage, is fairness or justice. In countries where there is endemic corruption, one is considered to be a bit of a misanthrope if you are not willing to pay a bribe to a traffic officer.

Any person in a position of authority over others also struggles with the issue of fairness. One cannot but help get on better with some people more than others. It is always easier to cultivate reciprocal relationships of generosity with people who you like. However, the struggle lies in staying fair with the whole group and not allowing your closeness to certain individuals to affect your impartiality. This is particularly at issue in dealing with disputes.

It suggests that being values-driven requires one to rise above the good opinion of others. Being values-driven requires us to do things because they are right, and not because they please others.

> **❛Being values-driven requires one to rise above the good opinion of others; it requires us to do things because they are right, and not because they please others.❜**

It is precisely because being values-driven sometimes requires us to act contrary to what will elicit the good opinion of others, that it requires courage.

When we examined the issue of power, we concluded that if I wanted your watch, your ability to withhold it gave you power over me. However, let's assume that I make such a fuss about the watch that you acquiesce and hand it over. Now I have the watch. The question is, can you still manipulate me, and clearly you can't, because you no longer have the watch. I now have it; it is in my control. This means that if I want things from someone, I can be manipulated by them, but only for as long as I don't have the thing in my hand. Once I have the thing in my hand, they lose their power over me.

You may say that you can still manipulate me because you can make me feel guilty that you have given me something. The assumption you will be making in this instance is that your opinion of me matters to me. If I truly could not care less that you thought I was a selfish individual, you really no longer have power over me.

However, assume I do not want the watch, but rather I want your good opinion of me. I want you to think that I am a good or a nice man. I clearly can never gain control over your good opinion of me like I can gain control over the watch, because your good opinion of me always stays with you. I cannot get my hands on it, so to speak. It always rests in your hands. This means that I am much more vulnerable to you when I want your good opinion than when I want things from you.

Being able to forgo my need for your watch requires generosity from me, because it requires me to rise above my need for things. Being able to forgo my need for your good opinion requires courage, because it requires me to be able to forgo my need for significance. Being able to forgo things is about generosity, being able to lose face (or self) is courage.

This means that we only really test someone's maturity by examining how they behave under pressure. A truly mature person will still do what is right when they are confronted by a situation where doing what is right and what is in their own interests is not the same. A further outcome of this is that we consider such people to be trustworthy.

> ❛ When you consider someone to be trustworthy, the assumption you make is that when the person is faced with a choice between the right thing to do and what is in their own self-interest, they will probably do what is right. ❜

When you consider someone to be trustworthy, the assumption you make is that when the person is faced with a choice between the right thing to do and what is in their own self-interest, they will probably do what is right.

When you do not find someone trustworthy, you are saying the opposite. You are of the view that when the person is faced with the distinction between what is right and what is expedient, they will do what is expedient.

> **'An irresponsible person will do what is expedient, and have no concern for the consequences for others.'**

It is for this reason that we connect maturity with responsibility. A responsible person is someone who can be trusted to do what is right, even if it does not suit them to do so. An irresponsible person will do what is expedient, and have no concern for the consequences for others.

The Immature and Mature World Views

The final thing that I would like to explore here is the perception of the world that underlies the different responses to it, by immature and mature people. A person who is needs-driven fundamentally constructs their intent in their day-to-day engagement with the world based on what they are getting from the world. It is as if they are saying to life 'you owe me'. It is therefore consistent with this way of looking at things, to be concerned with rights and a sense of entitlement.

A further implication of this immature view of things, is that the other is responsible. If you construct your engagement with the world based on what you are getting, you are fundamentally giving attention to what sits in the hands of the other, rather than what sits in your own hands. Because you only have control over what sits in your own hands, you feel out of control. You feel like a victim. You blame the other for the misfortunes in your life.

This sense of being the victim is entrenched by the response you solicit from the other. We agreed that if I construct my engagement with the other based on what I am getting from them, they are dangerous to me, and I am simultaneously dangerous to them. Remember that when two people are fundamentally dangerous to each other, it gives rise to conflict.

If my principal intent is to take, if follows that my average engagement with others will be to take, which, consequently, means that my average relationship will be cast in conflict. It will not be surprising that I will then inhabit a competitive world where I stagger from conflict to conflict, where I continually have to look after myself and to protect myself from others.

As a result, my view of the world will be that it is grounded in conflict; that survival is about succeeding at competing for limited resources. Every engagement with the other that is based on the intent to take, entrenches a sense of being alone and confronted by a hostile, dog-eat-dog world. One's experience of the world is, therefore, deeply alienating. The self is small and singular, and it is confronted by a multitude of competitors in a vast and hostile universe.

It is no wonder, then, that the self reacts with a sense of outrage. As a species, we are fundamentally fed up with being bullied. The problem is that we seek to blame the world, the people, the politicians, the governments or the churches for our sense of being oppressed. We do not understand that our experience of being victims is the product of our intent. When we seek to account for the reason that we feel so thwarted, that our sense of right is so outraged, we look at anything other than our own intent, which is the intent to take.

> **'...we seek to blame the world, the people, the politicians, the governments or the churches for our sense of being oppressed. We do not understand that our experience of being victims is the product of our intent. '**

It most certainly does not help that our intelligentsia has colluded to propagate a world view that treats survival of the fittest as the axiomatic first principle of all living systems, including human and social phenomena. But then again, maybe they are not to be blamed. They are as myopic as we are.

> **'** If your principal intent is to contribute, you are likely to engage most people on the basis of being helpful to them, and therefore, cultivate harmony with them ... you live in a social context where most people are your allies. **'**

They honestly have bought into the programme that self- interest is the only possible motive, however enlightened it may be. Nevertheless, in accepting their programme, we are sentencing ourselves, at best, to the spiritual maturity of a raging adolescent.

We have indicated that mature people base their engagement with the world on their responsibility in any given situation. They are fundamentally concerned with the value that is operative in the situation that they are in, with what they should be giving rather than with what they want to get. They therefore more often than not respond to the other on the basis of their duty in a situation, rather than their rights.

Dealing with the other on the basis of what the self should contribute creates conditions where the self and other are in harmony with each other. If your principal intent is to contribute, you are likely to engage most people on the basis of being helpful to them, and therefore, cultivate harmony with them. The cumulative effect of this is that you now live in a social context where most people are your allies.

Where an immature, self-interested and rights-focussed person perceives a battalion of enemies, a mature, duties-focussed individual becomes part of a battalion of allies. Shifting your intent from getting to giving is therefore consistent with trading an embattled life for a supported life, from a life where most engagements with other people are concerned with competition to one where they are most frequently concerned with co-operation.

Because maturation is a process, the shift from an immature experience of the world to a mature experience of the world is incremental.

While one looks at the world from a self-interested and taking point of view, you entrench the competitiveness of your engagement with the world, and hence your sense of alienation. By being here to take, you are saying both to the self and the other that the interests of the self and the other are discontinuous or in opposition. What is good for you must be bad for me, and vice versa.

> '...he who wins is not he who competes best, but he who co-operates best. '

Every time you act in the interest of the other, you are saying that their interest and yours are in accord. You are affirming a continuity that subsumes the interest of the self and the other. That affirmation of a continuity that carries both you and the other creates a sense of connectedness with the world. You are less and less of an alienated island battling it out in a sea of animosity and more of an organ in an organism. Just like it would be deeply problematic for your liver to compete with your body, it becomes deeply problematic for you to compete with your social world. Insofar as there is an incremental shift of your intent from being here to take to being here to give, there is a commensurately incremental shift of experience from a hostile to a friendly world.

You start seeing that he who wins is not he who competes best, but he who co-operates best. To claim this territory, you have to stand back from the individual and regard the system. If we view a given species in an ecosystem, then it would appear that the species competes. However, there is a symbiosis operative in any system that has to be the overarching rule, otherwise the system cannot be sustained. The rainforest is like my body. Just like the forest produces and eliminates things, so does my body.

> ‘You do not just broker lasting peace with your human brothers and sisters; you broker peace with the universe.’

Part of the maturation process is to engage in the work of reflection. It means that you do not look at the immediate and the apparent, but you take a step back and look at the overall system. That reflection requires one to take more into account than purely concrete sense perception. This implies that the experience of a friendly world is not merely a social world. You do not just broker lasting peace with your human brothers and sisters; you broker peace with the universe.

Our senses are set up to give us an appreciation of boundaries. We see and feel distinction. It appears to me that my body is a solid object that shares some of the characteristics of a chair. It has solid surfaces and limbs that exist independently from the environment. It is only once I examine the apparent self-sufficiency of these boundaries, that I come to recognise that the idea that they exist independently of the environment which they are in, is fictitious.

If I do not take in and give back to my environment continuously, in terms of food, excrement, oxygen and carbon monoxide, I die. In fact, when I examine this scaffold of a body that houses the flashlight of my consciousness, I recognise that it is constructed of the very same stuff the rest of the world is made up of. I do not exist independently of the world – I exist as part of the world. As exhalation empties the lungs sufficiently so that the next breath can be taken, so giving also empties the palm so that it can receive. A man who cultivates the habit of giving is identified with the continuity that flows through him.

Chapter 3

TRANSACTIONAL CORRECTNESS

We have demonstrated so far that both the process of maturation, and achieving the essence of what we aspire to, are products of the shift of intent from taking to giving. We have also suggested that this shift is incremental. For example, if we regard the intent to take as complete darkness and the intent to give as pure light, then most of us can describe our intent as various shades of grey. This means that at any given moment, we are confronted by two quite distinct variables: that which is concerned with what we want to get or take, and that which is concerned with what we should give. What changes as we mature, is the frequency with which we respond to the one or the other.

Most of us experience some sort of conflict between these contending possibilities, a conflict that causes us no end of trouble. Engaging in this struggle of clarifying our intent lies at the root of our maturation. The less mature we are, the more frequently we respond on the basis of what we want to take, and the more mature we are, the more our responses are based on what we should give. Let us explore the basic structure of both these intentions: the intent to take and the intent to give. One way of understanding the shift from the intent to take, to the intent to give, is that it is concerned with the inversion of means and ends. Assume, for example, that I am a boss with two subordinates, one called Joe and the other called Fred and furthermore that I am very experienced in a job they both have to do. One day I come to Joe and I say to him: 'Joe, in 1980 I did the job that you have to do now, so don't argue with me, just do what I did.' Joe is likely to become very annoyed with me. He will probably feel that I am bullying him.

	MEANS	ENDS	INTENT
JOE	PERSON	JOB	TAKE
FRED	JOB	PERSON	GIVE
	PERSON?	RESULT/JOB?	

On the other hand, if I tell Fred, 'Fred, in 1980 I did what you have to do and it worked. You may find it helpful to take a look at it,'

Fred is likely to be far more accepting of what I say. So what is the difference between the two?

At first it appears that the only difference between the two interactions is my behaviour. While Joe will probably think I am rude and feel that my approach is autocratic, Fred will most likely experience me as flexible and democratic.

While all of this is true, there is a further issue that be- comes apparent when one examines the pattern of means and ends in these two interactions. It is clear that if I say to Joe, 'Joe, in 1980 I did the job you have to do now, so don't argue with me, just do what I did,' then my principal aim in the interaction will be to achieve the same job or result that I achieved in 1980, and that I am using Joe as my means to achieve that outcome. Joe is my means to get the result I want.

On the other hand, if I tell Fred, 'Fred, in 1980 I did what you have to do and it worked. You may find it helpful to take a look at it,' I could have a completely different outcome from what I had in 1980. The outcome may even be a catastrophe. In this instance, my intention is to teach Fred something, and the job that is being done is the means I am using to teach him.

This suggests that when my intention shifts from being here to take to being here to give, there is an inversion of means and ends. When I am here to take from people, they are the means that I use to achieve the result I want from them. When I am here to give something to them, there is still an outcome, but I am using that outcome as an opportunity to give them something, or to contribute to them.

When I am here to take, my personal agenda is in the foreground; it is the centre of my attention. It is the thing that I am after, and the other is my means to satisfy that agenda. When I am here to give someone something, their agenda sits in the foreground of my attention, and the outcome that I am trying to manage through them becomes the means through which I satisfy that agenda.

This suggests that in the first instance, transactional correctness means acting consistently with what is in the best interest of the other in the situation that you are in, irrespective of the outcome you are trying to manage. It implies an ability to forgo the outcome in the interest of acting in the best interest of the other. Conversely, it is transactionally incorrect when you use people as the means to achieve an outcome.

> ❛ When I am here to take from people, they are the means that I use to achieve the result I want from them. When I am here to give something to them, there is still an outcome, but I am using that outcome as an opportunity to give them something, or to contribute to them. ❜

Transactional Correctness and Action

What is already apparent about the intent to give is that it is not just about doing what is pleasing to the other. It is based on action that is in the best interest of the other. It is therefore appropriate to think of such action as giving the situation its due. We argued that the primary attribute of giving each situation its due has a feeling of kindness to it.

TRANSACTIONAL CORRECTNESS	
	ACTION
SECONDARY ELEMENT	COURAGE *(Cowardice)*
PRIMARY ELEMENT	GENEROSITY *(Selfishness)*
ROOT	GIVING EACH SITUATION ITS DUE *(Expediency)*

It is concerned with being able to suspend one's own agenda for the agenda of the other. It is about being generous. However, it is also apparent that if you give alcohol to an alcoholic, even though he demands it, you are not acting in his best interest. In such an instance, you have to be courageous enough to withhold the bottle. Giving is not about being nice; it is about being appropriate. It means consistently acting with the courage or generosity that is operative in each particular situation.

The opposite of giving each situation its due, is to act with expediency. In other words, not basing your actions on what the situation demands, but merely what is convenient or suits you at the time. We also established that an illogical and inappropriate application of generosity or courage leads to two forms of taking: selfishness (acting in a so-called courageous manner when generosity is called for) and cowardice (acting generously when the situation demands courage).

Transactional Correctness and Reflection

It is only possible to give a situation its due if you appraise the situation correctly – if you see the situation as it is. Seeing things as they are clearly precedes giving each situation its due. In the previous chapter we concluded that Ayesha would have been selfish if she had slapped the child who asked her for food. However, if she had, it would be interesting to explore Ayesha's motivations. She could, for instance, justify her behaviour by arguing that the child was something other than he had presented himself to be. Perhaps asking for food was a ruse to see what he could steal, or maybe he was just playing the fool with her. Regardless of which explanation she offers, it means that she had a presumption about the situation and, as a result, did not act appropriately. So we see that you can't act appropriately when you presume, because you are not seeing things as they really are.

TRANSACTIONAL CORRECTNESS		
	REFLECTION	**ACTION**
ROOT	SEEING THINGS AS THEY ARE (Presumption)	GIVING EACH SITUATION ITS DUE (Expediency)

The next question is whether the logic runs the other way as well: If seeing things as they are enables giving each situation its due, does giving each situation its due then also enable seeing things as they are? I believe it does.

An example that comes to mind most immediately is what happens to people in domestic disputes. Assume John has a flaming row with his wife.

Instead of saying goodbye to her, he fires off a few hurtful parting shots and storms out of the house. He bullies his way through the traffic and arrives at work, still hot under the collar. His secretary greets him, and he grunts a curt reply.

John has not been appropriate in his interaction with the secretary. In fact, he has been rude, and the question is why? He misbehaved in the spat with his wife; he said things he should not have said. He spent the whole journey in the car justifying his behaviour and rehearsing to himself the litany of injustices that his wife has subjected him to. When he arrives at work, his body is in the office, but in his mind he is still continuing the argument with his wife. He is not present and does not see things as they are because his attention is stuck in an unresolved drama.

> ' When you behave inappropriately, it keeps some of your attention trapped in the previous encounter, and you are therefore not available in the next one. '

When you behave inappropriately, it keeps some of your attention trapped in the previous encounter, and you are therefore not available in the next one. This is even truer when you were cowardly. Very often the things that you rehearse to yourself in the car are not the things you actually said, but the things you did not say, either because you were too angry at the time, or you were too frightened.

We can, therefore, conclude that acting solely on the basis of what the situation requires of you – giving the situation its due – is an inadequate rule for understanding what it means to be transactionally correct. Appropriate action is based on an appropriate appraisal of the situation. Seeing things as they are and giving each situation its due are mutually enabling components of transactional correctness. Seeing things as they are enables you to identify what the situation you are faced with requires of you. When you base your actions on that insight, it enables you to change and to take the next step forward in growth.

Gratitude, Trust and Seeing Things as They Are

We have argued that giving each situation its due has two attributes, namely generosity and courage. We have also argued that giving each situation its due is based on an inward, reflective element, namely seeing things as they are. The question that follows is: what are the inward, reflective equivalents of generosity and courage?

Gratitude and Generosity

The inward equivalent of generosity is gratitude. Gratitude implies that you recognise that you have received in excess of your due. When you entertain that view, it is easy for you to give away. You recognise that there is an abundance of benevolence in the world, and you do not need to be miserly. Should you be of the view that you can account for your good fortune on the basis of your ingenuity alone, you will perceive your good fortune as the result of a transactional account. This means that you will discount the possibility of abundance in the world. You will never see anything given, as given to give away. You will see it as part of a transaction. True generosity, however, means to give for the sake of giving, and not making an investment in the hope of ensuring some future reward.

Gratitude means that you have received more than you have earned. It is this attribute that enables you to give unconditionally; to be generous.

If gratitude means that I accept I have been given in excess of my due, then the inverse of gratitude has to be resentment. When I am resentful, I am of the view that what has happened to me is unjust. I have received less than my due. Should I carry this conviction within me, it will be very difficult for me to give anything to anyone else. I will not see myself as being here to give; I will see myself as being owed. I will therefore not be able to be generous.

> **True generosity means to give for the sake of giving, and not making an investment in the hope of ensuring some future reward.**

An interesting implication of this, is that the claim to self-sufficiency produces resentment. The claim to self-sufficiency implies that I think I am the master of my own good fortune and that I account for my good circumstances on the basis of my own ingenuity. I have been given nothing; I have earned all the good things I have. This view will translate into a desire to see balanced reciprocity in every engagement, because I live in a world where nothing is given unreservedly.

> **The claim to self-suficiency means that I will constantly seek to guarantee outcomes.**

Because a one-on-one reciprocation very rarely happens, I am frequently likely to feel short-changed and resentful. The claim to self- sufficiency also means that I will constantly seek to guarantee outcomes. Gratitude and generosity are mutually enabling. As gratitude enables generosity, so generosity enables gratitude. When someone is a generous person they are able to give unconditionally – they give to give away. They know this is possible, because they have done it themselves. When such a person sees someone else being generous, they will therefore not necessarily assume that the other person is making an investment. They will see it as it is; they will see a generous act. This implies that their own generosity enables them to recognise the generosity of others, and it is the recognition of the generosity of the other that produces gratitude.

Trust and Courage

The inner equivalent of courage is trust, which is very nicely illustrated in the following game that is frequently played in a team-building context: Imagine that we have a group of people standing in a circle with a blindfolded person standing in the middle. Imagine that we ask the blindfolded person to fall, promising that we will catch her. Clearly, the ease with which she falls, is directly related to the degree to which she trusts the people standing in the circle.

We will also find that, provided the blindfolded person is caught before she falls, the most difficult time for her to fall will be the very first time. After that, she will incrementally trust more and will fall with greater ease each time. In the very first fall, she will not really know if she can trust the group. She would have to take the courageous step to fall in order to learn if she can trust the group. Acting courageously enables her trust.

Once the blindfolded person discovers that she can trust the group, it will be a lot easier for her to take the courageous step of falling a second time. As her courage enables her trust, so her trust enables her courage.

TRANSACTIONAL CORRECTNESS		
	REFLECTION	**ACTION**
SECONDARY ELEMENT	TRUST (Distrust)	COURAGE (Cowardice)
PRIMARY ELEMENT	GRATITUDE (Resentment)	GENEROSITY (Selfishness)
ROOT	SEEING THINGS AS THEY ARE (Presumption)	GIVING EACH SITUATION ITS DUE (Expediency)

Conversely, should the blindfolded person's distrust of the situation override her trust completely, it will be impossible for her to take the courageous step of falling. It will create a situation where the person will behave in a fearful way that will make it impossible for her to trust the group.

The Primacy of Gratitude

Of the four elements of transactional correctness, namely gratitude, generosity, trust and courage, gratitude has pride of place as being the most significant and causal category. This becomes apparent when one considers the orientation of these elements in terms of time.

The primary elements of gratitude and generosity are orientated to the past. When you are grateful, you are grateful for something that has happened. When you are generous, you are able to give away what you accumulated in the past. The secondary elements of trust and courage are orientated to the future. When I trust, I trust that all will be well. When I am courageous, I face the barbarians as they come toward me over the hill. Both of these elements are forward looking, to the future.

Should my appraisal of the past be steeped in resentment, it will be very difficult for me to be generous. Why should I give anything to anyone who has wronged me?

My resentment about what happened to me in the past, will also create a sense of distrust when I look forward. After all, if they have wronged me once, why would they not do it again?

> ❛ The funda-mental trick to transactional correctness and cultivating the intent to give, is to learn how to deal with your own resentment. ❜

This distrust will make it impossible for me to take a risk with someone and act courageously.

This implies that the fundamental trick to transactional correctness and cultivating the intent to give, is to learn how to deal with your own resentment. Of all the skills that enable the achievement of security, fulfilment, power and harmony, the skill of knowing how to transmute resentment into gratitude, is pre-eminent. A key to this process is to honestly face your own resentment and ingratitude.

If giving each situation its due means acting with generosity and courage, and seeing things as they are means viewing things with gratitude and trust, it has to mean that if you are not looking at the past with gratitude, you are not seeing things as they are. Similarly, if you are not looking at the future with trust, you are also doing violence to the truth.

The following section examines this potentially contentious view

Transactional Correctness and the Social Other

What the blindfolded falling exercise helps to demonstrate, is that the categories of transactional correctness are not only operative between one's own inward and outward, they are also operative between the self and the social other. Your inner condition is reflected in the relationships around you.

We see that the exercise is concerned with trust. The blindfolded person in the middle has to trust the people in the circle. At the same time, for the exercise to succeed, the people on the periphery have to take responsibility. They are, by implication, saying to the blindfolded person, 'Trust us. We are responsible. We will not let you fall.'

To take responsibility is a courageous thing to do. It is saying that when you look into the future, you will prove yourself worthy of the trust that is invested in you. You will step up to the plate; you will not let the side down. It is true that the blindfolded person has to trust the people in the circle, but if those people do not have the courage to take responsibility, the exercise will fail. The courage of the people in the circle enables the trust of the blindfolded person.

At the same time, it is the trust of the blindfolded person that enables the courage of the people in the circle. If the blindfolded person does not trust them enough, the people in the circle will not be able to demonstrate that they can be responsible. If the blindfolded person does not trust the people in the circle, she could possibly take a check-step to ensure that she is not dropped. This attempt to control the outcome will make the trajectory of her fall unpredictable, making it more likely that the people in the circle will fumble and drop her, thereby proving her view that they cannot be trusted.

It is also true that the people in the circle are generous with the blindfolded person. Once she has fallen a few times and been caught, her appropriate response to the people in the circle would be gratitude that she has not been dropped.

When the self recognises the generosity of the other, the self is grateful, while the gratitude of the self enables the generosity of the other. It is a pleasure to give to someone who is genuinely grateful, and an annoyance to give to someone who is resentful and has a sense of entitlement.

In fact, a sense of entitlement in the self changes the nature of the giving of the other. If I feel entitled, I consider myself owed. If the other feels compelled to give, it is not a free giving of their abundance and they are not truly being generous. Generosity has to be a choice.

TRANSACTIONAL CORRECTNESS		
	REFLECTION	**ACTION**
ATTRIBUTE	SUBMISSION *(Rebellion)*	POWER *(Control)*
SECONDARY ELEMENT	TRUST *(Distrust)*	COURAGE *(Cowardice)*
PRIMARY ELEMENT	GRATITUDE *(Resentment)*	GENEROSITY *(Selfishness)*
ROOT	SEEING THINGS AS THEY ARE *(Presumption)*	GIVING EACH SITUATION ITS DUE *(Expediency)*

When I feel compelled to give, I am, in fact, not giving, but being taken from. The gratitude of the self enables the generosityofthe other. The trust of the self enables the courage of the other.

Should I wish to live among people who are my allies, the key work I have to do, is to find what there is to be grateful for and let that inform my trust of others. The question remains, however, whether it is naïve to view the social other through such rose-coloured lenses.

If I see things as they are, I will recognise that the social other has given me immeasurably more than my due. None of the modern conveniences that I now take for granted would have existed had it not been for the collective human endeavour and inventiveness since time immemorial.

Take the shirt that you're wearing today, for example. Very long ago, almost thirty-thousand years back, people discovered that you could take plant fibres and spin them into yarn. Sometime later others discovered that you could weave yarn into fabric, and quite recently, a few centuries ago, English engineers invented large mechanical looms, thereby making it possible to mass produce fibre-based fabrics. All this collective ingenuity just to put a shirt on my back, and not a single cent of royalty fees charged!

I would like to cite another example to demonstrate this point. I was the son of immigrants and went to Afrikaans schools in the 1960s. I would consider my mother tongue to be Afrikaans. Having had this background, I was also not immune to the prejudices of that community. One of the prejudices I inherited was a visceral hostility toward the English.

About a decade ago, I was invited to make a contribution to a Manufacturing Leaders' Programme at Cambridge. As I stood in the room waiting to start the day's training, the irrationality of my prejudice against the English struck me like a blow from a mallet. There I was, being allowed in their academic holy of holies, to teach my stuff. I was doing so in English, not just because they were English, but also because it would be impossible to do what I do in Afrikaans. My Afrikaans is just not good enough, and English provides such a fantastic vocabulary to do this sort of thing.

> **'**None of the modern conveniences that I now take for granted would have existed had it not been for the collective human endeavour and inventiveness since time immemorial. **'**

> **'For a modern human being, no matter how underprivileged, to look at the social other with resentment, is not to see things as they are.'**

The English language, as we know it today, is the product of a spontaneous collaborative process that spans millennia. The Romans had a hand in it, as did the Greeks, the Germans, the Scandinavians, and the French. Not a single one of these people has demanded one cent's worth of royalties. All this collective ingenuity bequeathed to me, free, and I respond by being resentful toward the people who speak it as their mother tongue? Astonishing!

If I worked as a slave for the rest of my life, I could never repay the collective genius that put the shirt on my back, never mind repay the gift of the language I speak. If we see things as they are, we will know that we stand on the shoulders of giants. For a modern human being, no matter how underprivileged, to look at the social other with resentment, is not to see things as they are. The collective human genius that stands between where we are now in the twenty first century and our earliest homo sapiens ancestors, is a gift of truly stupendous proportions.

Transactional Correctness and the Attributes of Power and Submission

A person with allies has power, while a person without allies is weak. When the social other is your ally, you are in harmony with them; when they are your enemy, you are in conflict with them. In our earlier exploration of harmony, and our discussion around the examples of Joe and Fred, it became apparent that the price of soliciting the good will and alliance of the other is to deliberately suspend your own agenda for their agenda in the situation that you are in. You have to yield or submit your interests. Paradoxically, the price of power is submission.

One of the implications of this is that the self can never own power. The other always grants power. As soon as the self seeks to claim power, it corrupts to control. I am powerful when you do what I require you to do because you want to do so. If you do what I require because you have to, I am using some form of compulsion. I am invoking a mechanism of control. That control makes you hostile to me, and I lose your good will. I lose the alliance. I lose power. For me to retain your alliance, I have to forgo my agenda and entrust it to you. I do so by unconditionally submitting myself to what would genuinely be in your best interest.

The opposite of submission is rebellion. When I refuse to subordinate my agenda to the agenda of the other, I am in a state of rebellion against things as they are.

That rebellion is translated into an intent to compel the other to deliver what I want; it has the intent to control. We see now why a humble demeanour is so universally prized as an attribute of good citizenship.

Just as giving does not imply being nice, submission does not imply always being compliant. The submission that we are referring to here is the submission to what is truly appropriate for the other. If it is in the other's best interest that I confront them, then that confrontation is not rebellion; it would be an act of submission, although the submission will be expressed as a challenge and a negation. Any person who has had a positive relationship with a sports coach would understand what I am referring to here. Good coaches are not always nice people. They can be irascible or mean. However, when an athlete understands that this behaviour is an expression of the intent of the coach to bring out the best possible in the athlete, the athlete stays loyal to the coach.

> ❛The self can never own power. The other always grants power. As soon as the self seeks to claim power, it corrupts to control. ❜

There is no question that a parent should always act in the best interests of the child. However, acting in the best interests of the child clearly does not mean acquiescing to whatever the child wants. It is precisely because we have got this wrong that we now live in a world populated by obese, sugar-addicted and discourteous brats.

Transactional Correctness and Awe

We fundamentally have two relationships with the other: The first is with the social other, that is, other people. The second is with the totality of the other. The totality of the other is everything that is presented to you in the moment you are in. The social other is always a subset of this totality. Even if you were standing in a crowd, it is unlikely that people will fill the whole picture that you would see. There would also be some sky, a few trees or some buildings. The social other will always remain a subset of the totality of the other.

Our relationship with the totality of the other is our primary relationship. People may come and go, but while you are alive, the fact remains that you will always have other than you as your consistent, inescapable companion. The transactional rules that operate between your own inward and outward, as well as your relationship with the social other, also operate in your engagement with the totality of the other.

To see things as they are must mean to recognise that the totality of the other has given wildly, immeasurably in excess of your due. You and your intent are housed in a vessel of attention.

SOCIAL OTHER

THE TOTALITY OF THE OTHER

This vessel is like a light that shines out onto the world. The light is housed on the scaffold of your body. This scaffold has come from other than you; you clearly did not make it.

If you examine what it has taken for your body to be here, you would see that all events prior to now have conspired to make it possible. From the Big Bang there has been a careful weaving together of events over immeasurable aeons that finally produced this incredible, unlikely you.

This weaving together continues moment to moment. You cannot produce, out of your own body, what is necessary to sustain you. My ability to write these words is powered by my breakfast, which included some toast and some cheese. Where did that come from?

TRANSACTIONAL CORRECTNESS		
	REFLECTION	**ACTION**
ESSENCE	AWE *(Terror)*	SIGNIFICANCE *(Arrogance)*
ATTRIBUTE	SUBMISSION *(Rebellion)*	POWER *(Control)*
SECONDARY ELEMENT	TRUST *(Distrust)*	COURAGE *(Cowardice)*
PRIMARY ELEMENT	GRATITUDE *(Resentment)*	GENEROSITY *(Selishness)*
ROOT	SEEING THINGS AS THEY ARE *(Presumption)*	GIVING EACH SITUATION ITS DUE *(Expediency)*

Well, the farmer sowed the wheat that drew into itself water and minerals from the soil, light from the sun and carbon dioxide from the air. It wove these things together to produce the grain that I ate. The story of the cheese is even more complex.

So in me, there is also not me. There is other than me. There is grain, there are minerals, there is sunlight, there is water and there is milk. My capacity to metabolise what I ate, the result of rain, sun and earth on wheat seed, the effect of heat on flour – are a tiny subset of the infinite number of blessings that sustain me. I am a gift to me by other than me. I am a gift to me from the totality of the other.

I recognise this and I am grateful, because it is apparent to me that I am the undeserving recipient of largesse of unfathomably vast generosity. I also recognise that the generosity that has sustained me has nothing to do with my own ingenuity. I therefore have reason to believe that this largesse will continue, irrespective of what I do, now or in the future.

Since it has been there for me in the past, I must trust that it will be there for me in the future. Besides, should it not be there, there is precious little I can do about it. If I stop being a focus for this weaving-together of good fortune by the totality of the other, I will die. This totality of the other is my creator, sustainer and destroyer. It is my superordinate Lord. All power sits there, and, in the final analysis, I am the submitted, whether I acknowledge this or not.

I find it inconceivable that this weaving together of good fortune that has produced me, and continues to produce me, is the product of arbitrary accidents. In the very design of the scaffold that my attention sits on, I recognise a deliberateness that I attribute to the totality of the other, because this scaffold has come from the totality of the other.

I stand in a deliberate, personal and conscious relationship with the totality of the other, who is the fundamental nourishing, enabling and succouring dance partner of my life.

When I recognise this deliberateness, I cannot but wonder why. To what end has other than me made this stupendous investment in me? Why was this courageous risk taken to make this incredible investment that produced me? Why did the totality of the other conspire to produce the perceiver? The only reasonable answer that occurs to me, is the perceiver was produced to perceive. So what is it that the perceiver perceives?

We have been arguing that the inner equivalent of giving each situation its due, is to see things as they are. To see is to perceive. So what is it that we perceive when we see things as they are? In order to explore this question, we need to afford ourselves the opportunity to gain a sense of perspective, so we can get a good view of how things are. I suggest, therefore, that you join me at the top of a very high mountain, so that we can get a good view.

As we stand here, on top of this very high mountain, the first impression we get is one of scale. We are miniscule creatures compared with the vastness of all

> ❛I stand in a deliberate, personal and conscious relationship with the totality of the other, who is the fundamental nourishing, enabling and succouring dance partner of my life. ❜

that. That vastness remains there, even if we should retreat behind the walls of the city, or behind the inward walls of internal chatter that drags our attention away from the vastness. However, just because we are not looking, does not mean to say the vastness has disappeared.

When that which is very small regards that which is vast beyond comparison, there is only one of two possible responses: The first is terror and the second is awe. Awe is possible when that which is small, recognises that this vastness he perceives is somehow benevolently disposed to him. It is not his foe, it is his ally.

> ❛I have been made by other than me to be amazed by, in love with, enchanted and in awe of other than me. This experience vindicates the investment made in me. This is why I am human. ❜

When I recognise that all which is not me has conspired to produce me so that I can regard it, then I am in a state of deep and transcendental awe. I have been made by other than me to be amazed by, in love with, enchanted and in awe of other than me. This experience vindicates the investment made in me. This is why I am human.

My awe, however, is a choice. I can look out at the vastness without having this reflection and just see that which is vast and wild. Whether deliberate or not, it is the nature of that which is vast, wild, unassailable and arbitrary to annihilate that which is small, ordered and vulnerable. If I do not confer a deliberately benign intelligence on the other side of perception, I can only quake in terror. This terror will invoke in me a sense of outraged rebellion. I will seek to control this madness. I will do whatever I need to do to stay alive. I will be risk averse, precisely because of my heightened awareness of danger. I will find it difficult to trust. I will constantly seek to guarantee my good fortune because I will be deeply suspicious of any possibility that the other could be my ally.

Above all, at the root of my experience there will be the seething discontentment of a small being, slapped around by arbitrary fate. My response will be to hide behind the outer walls of the city and the inner walls of words.

To be sure, we collude with our brothers to weave an illusion of security in this vastness. We build cities, we protect ourselves behind the walls of language. We somehow delude ourselves that we can hold out against all that is out there if we can at least be good to each other. This attempt is futile.

If I am fundamentally suspicious of life, there is precious little I can do to prevent that suspicion from seeping into my relationships with others. After all, the social other remains a subset of the totality of the other. If suspicion becomes the unconscious wallpaper of my inner life, it will be virtually impossible for that not to manifest in my relationships. So, in the deepest sense, without faith, no morality is possible.

The last observation I would like to make here is: the importance of recognising that the social other does not operate in abstraction from the totality of the other. The social other will always be part of the totality of the other, but as a small and subordinate subset.

> ' If suspicion becomes the unconscious wallpaper of my inner life, it will be virtually impossible for that not to manifest in my relationships. So, in the deepest sense, without faith, no morality is possible. '

Chapter 4

THE FOUR INTENTIONS

We concluded previously that the process of maturation is concerned with the process of the maturation of the intent to give unconditionally. This is an incremental process from absolute immaturity (being here to get unconditionally) to absolute maturity (being here to give unconditionally). The proportional composition of our intent to get or give, changes as e mature.

If, using a metaphor of shade, you view being here to get as absolute darkness, and being here to give as absolute light, it implies that, in between these two extremes, you will find a gradient of various shades of grey. This concept enables us to delineate more epochs (stages or periods) than purely that which is immature or mature. If we reduce the increments to a fractional equation, one can describe four stages in the maturation of intent:

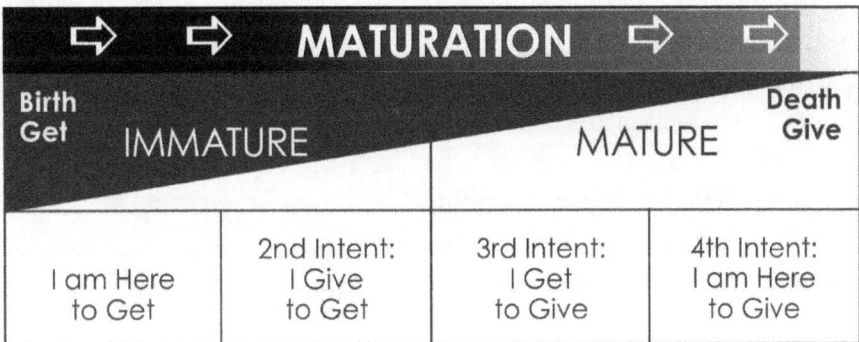

⇨ ⇨ MATURATION ⇨ ⇨			
Birth Get IMMATURE		MATURE **Death Give**	
I am Here to Get	2nd Intent: I Give to Get	3rd Intent: I Get to Give	4th Intent: I am Here to Give

First Intent: More than 75% darkness in the gradient. The phrasing of this intent would be,
'I am here to get.'
Second Intent: Between 75% and 50% darkness in the gradient -
'I give to get.'
Third Intent: Between 50% and 75% light in the gradient -
'I get to give'.
Fourth Intent: Between 75% and 100% light in the gradient
'I am here to give'.

Before we explore these stages or epochs in more detail, it is important to note that using this fractional approach to understanding maturation is simply a useful metaphor and should by no means be seen as a scientifically proven instrument. In presenting this model, I seek to craft a useful description of something which can only be treated in broad brush strokes, because when dealing with issues of intent, you are dealing with subtle matters that cannot readily be reduced to the same order of phenomena as the volume of a kilogram of water at sea level.

First Intent: I am Here to Get

Having had close encounters of a quite extended nature with a number of infants in my life, I have come to the rather politically incorrect conclusion that a newborn can be most accurately described as a digestive tract with two eyes plonked on top. The whole of life seems to be a continuous process of ingesting and evacuating, and any attendant adults are purely the facilitators of this affair.

In fact, describing the attending adults as facilitators probably does not accurately reflect the infant's experience. When describing someone as a facilitator, one describes someone who is recognised as having some deliberate and conscious agency, whereas I very much doubt the infant has that view of his or her mother. It appears to me that the infant

1st Intent
GREED
I am here to get.
All is Function.

experiences its mother as somehow indivisibly connected with itself. The reason for this is there is very little delay between the expression of a need and the satisfaction thereof, which would create an impression that self and other (or mother), are the same.

> ‘Mother is not experienced as other; mother is experienced as self, as continuous with and connected to self, as one with self. ’

I know, for example, that my hand and my head are somehow connected because when I have an itch on my head my hand can quite spontaneously scratch the itch. I do not have to go through a complex manoeuvre to get my hand to scratch the itch. I just intend for my head to be scratched and my hand rushes to the rescue.

The same can be said for the experience of the infant's connection with its mother. First little Suzie bawls her discontentment at being hungry and, quick as a flash, something wet and warm gets put into her mouth. Then she has cramps, so she gets paced around the room on her angelic mother's shoulder until she paints the shoulder with some- thing objectionable.

After a short nap, she awakes grunting and produces the final product of her metabolic process. This part of the process does not necessarily require bawling to solicit help – the smell more often than not does the trick.

It appears to me inconceivable that little Suzie is thinking, 'I must now get mother to feed me,' or 'I must now get her to clean my bottom'. What appears to going on is a far more unconscious process somewhat like my hand and my head. In other words, mother is not experienced as other; mother is experienced as self, as continuous with and connected to self, as one with self. Should one explicitly frame an intent from what one observes, then it does not seem to occur to Suzie that she needs to do anything to get what she wants. She therefore does not have to give anything to get. She gets what she wants with very little deliberate management of the other. She is here to get, quite unconditionally and unashamedly.

This getting is principally about very crude or basic needs. It is not about listening to a Shakespearian sonnet. It is therefore helpful to describe this epoch or stage as the epoch of greed. It is the epoch where basic functional and metabolic issues take centre stage. All is function and the other is an appendage to facilitate that function.

Unfortunately, this idyllic state of affairs does not continue into perpetuity. Over time,there is a definite change with regard to the closeness of the mothering. On occasion the wet and warm stuff does not arrive as soon as it was wanted, or some other object of delight does not seem to be forthcoming. Also, little Suzie has discovered some of her own agency. She can waddle up to the table and reach for the apple. Although still very clumsy, she starts to understand that you can do things to get what you want.

This growth of an experience of independent agency comes at the price of an insight into the rather upsetting truth, which is that other, or mother, are not quite the same as the self. They are disconnected. They are separate, and therefore are able to withhold the good auspices of the self. The experience of this appears to be outrageous for little Suzie. How dare they think they cannot do what I demand of them! We have been transported to the world of little Mussolini, the world of the toddler. If they have the gall to withhold what you want, then scream blue murder until they acquiesce.

> ❝ This getting is principally about very crude or basic needs .. It is the epoch of greed. It is the epoch where basic functional and metabolic issues take centre stage. ❞

> ‘What is most intimidating about children during this phase of their lives is that they know no subtlety. They do not like; they either love or they hate. ’

As always, it is useful to cite one's own experience in these matters. My eldest son, Khalil, was in this phase otherwise referred to as 'the terrible twos' when I started my business in 1990. It was a very challenging and anxious time for me, as I was attempting to start a consulting business as a 30-year-old in a market that was in the throes of a developing civil war.

For me, one of the great pleasures of life at the time was to buy a chocolate for Khalil on my way home from work. He reacted so nicely! As I drew up in the carport, I would see him waddling down the garden path, beaming from ear to ear in eager expectation of the chocolate which I would normally give him as I got out of the car. By the time we got to the front door, there was chocolate on him and me. He was simply delightful, my little boy!

However, on occasion I would have a nightmarish day at work and I would forget his treat. When that happened, Khalil would fly into a rage. He would fling himself to the ground in a fit of temper and bellow his outrage at me as loudly as his little lungs could manage; quite appalling. What is most intimidating about children during this phase of their lives is that they know no subtlety. They do not like; they either love or they hate.

There had been a number of repeat performances of this drama, and it seemed like he was getting his conditioning of me licked. One day, however, I was driving home and as I passed the shops, the thought occurred to me that I should not forget his sweet. This thought was followed hotly by a second thought, which was that I was allowing myself to be bullied by a two-year-old. I could feel my jaw set. To hell with him, I thought. No more chocolates.

When I arrived home, he once again came waddling down the garden path, clearly anticipating his sweet. I got out of the car a bit more abruptly than normal, the set still in my jaw. He took one look at my face, waddled up and said 'Daddy!' as he hugged my leg. What had become apparent to him seemed to be something like the following: 'If I scream at him today, then tomorrow I won't get a sweet. If I want a sweet from him tomorrow, I had better be nice to him today.' What had happened to him was a momentous shift of his intent – a shift of that we could call the Second Intent.

The Second Intent: I Give to Get

If one could have gained access to what was going on in little Khalil's head one would have witnessed his first tentative steps into delaying gratification to achieve outcomes beneficial to himself – an understanding that he had to give in order to get. This delay of gratification was associated with the insight that his good outcomes sat with the other, and that the other had the power to withhold them. This epoch in one's life can therefore be described as the epoch of fear, because it is about the concern that the self is beholden to the other and that the other has the power to withhold what the self wants.

1st Intent	2nd Intent
GREED	FEAR
I am here to get.	I give to get.
All is Function.	Meaning is functional.

The first manifestation of the in-tent to give in order to get produces the compliance of the pre-teen child.

Little Suzie has discovered that if you don't eat the marshmallow now, that if you do as they ask and resist eating it, they will give you two, later on. She has become daddy's darling. He can do no wrong in her eyes. She knows just what to do and say to melt his heart. In this period of our lives we are most compliant. Our emotional life also gains some subtlety. Now Suzie can do something a bit more nuanced than just love or hate. She can like.

Don't be fooled, though. This development is not because she has suddenly discovered a profound inner life and has given herself over to reflecting on the subtleties of things like love, compassion and justice. What has really happened here is that she has discovered that being kind, sweet, loving and compliant has a very pragmatic benefit. She is willing to entertain issues of meaning because they have a functional implication; you learn to be nice because it works to be nice.

> ❛ Being kind, sweet, loving and compliant have a very pragmatic beneit ... Issues of meaning have a functional implication; you learn to be nice because it works to be nice. ❜

We all love pre-teen kids. They are enchanting. We have no idea of the ride of rage that is lurking around the corner. At 12 years and 364 days, your sweet little child goes to bed. The next day, on her thirteenth birthday, a monster emerges from her room that is so unrecognisable that you cannot help asking 'Who are you and what have you done with my daughter?'

Overnight the sweet compliance of her childhood has gone, only to be replaced by the cocky, opinionated competitiveness of an adolescent. Suzie has discovered that it is not good enough merely to be liked. She has learned that if you are always nice so that they like you, they stop taking you seriously. Actually what you should be, is be important. If they consider you significant, then they will take you seriously and you will get what you want.

The phrasing of an adolescent's intent is like a pre-teen, it is still 'I give to get'. However, now the deep zero-sum game that the phrasing implies comes to its full fruition. This results in interactions that are more often than not win/lose interactions. The adolescent becomes mired in conflict, and there are very few relationships that escape these hostilities.

All things are reduced to a competition and a cause for conflict. At one point, we had four adolescent boys under the same roof, and I can still point out the scars borne by the house as a result. At the drop of a hat a stray remark could spark a fight of truly epic proportions. In the course of this fight, it is absolutely futile to attempt to get the disputing parties to see reason. Their rage is far too hormone-fuelled to enable that to happen.

Even if these interactions do not result in open warfare, the adolescent is still continuously negotiating with others in order to ensure that there is a *quid pro quo* benefit for every interaction. This results in a very large proportion of interactions with the other having the character of a negotiation.

The problem with these negotiations is that they are rarely concerned with being able to compare like with like. In the mind of the adolescent, there is always an inkling of being short-changed. This discontent easily spills over into a depressed lassitude, where very few things seem worth it. There is resentment regarding things that have to be done in order to achieve outcomes. They are the difficult price you have to pay, the suffering you have to endure to get what you want. So your life becomes suffering. Probably the most objectionable quality of people in this epoch of their lives is their narcissism. The competitiveness of the condition solicits a very unflattering fascination with everything about the self. Healthy adolescents speak about themselves, take selfies, admire themselves surreptitiously in shop windows and get up to other rather

> ' In the mind of the adolescent, there is always an inkling of being short-changed. This discontent easily spills over into a depressed lassitude, where very few things seem worth it. '

embarrassing capers because they know that they really are the best, and they know that others don't know that.

> The self realises that anything that is based on win/lose becomes lose/lose in the fullness of time. If I really want their admiration and afirmation, I have to genuinely seek to act in their interest.

Mercifully, people do not stay like this forever. Toward late adolescence, the flaw in competitive motive is grasped, albeit intuitively. When you compete, you establish win/lose engagements with others in order to win. Clearly for you to win, the other person has to lose; this is a zero-sum game. It becomes apparent that this is problematic when you consider why you wish to win. Clearly, the intent to win is concerned with becoming admired by others; seen to be significant by others.

When one seeks to achieve this admiration by winning or competing with them, what you are really saying is, 'I want your love and I intend to get it by degrading you'. By late adolescence, it becomes apparent that nobody likes a person who has humiliated them. The competition that you engage in produces exactly the opposite of what you want. Rather than gaining affirmation and admiration, you achieve negation and derision. The self realises that anything that is based on win/lose becomes lose/lose in the fullness of time. If I really want their admiration and affirmation, I have to genuinely seek to act in their interest. This is the birth of the 3rd Intent.

The Third Intent: I Get to Give

The first glimmering of the Third Intent becomes apparent when, out of the blue, a person develops a social conscience. This sense of conscience is very attractive in young adults, but it can also make them vulnerable, particularly to throwing themselves into grand acts of magnanimity. Young Suzie goes to university and throws herself into a campaign to stop rhino poaching. More distressingly, these days, young Farid surreptitiously boards a plane to the Levant to join ISIS.

It is interesting that it is never the bearded old codgers propagating a Wahhabi (Islamic fundamentalist) remodelling of the world, who end up in a suicide vest.

1st Intent	2nd Intent	3rd Intent
GREED	FEAR	GENEROSITY
I am here to get.	I give to get.	I get to give.
All is Function.	Meaning is functional.	Function is meaningful.

It is always the young, bright-eyed recruit. It is the young recruit who buys into the agenda of committing the grand sacrificial act to fix the world, once and for all.

It is as if we all go through a millenarian* phase in our maturation process, where the simple solutions that are going to fix the world, are painfully apparent to us and when we are convinced that the noble sacrifice of the few will achieve such an end. We are quite willing to, proverbially, burn down the village, kill the cattle and destroy the crops to enable the New World to arise. (*Millenarians believe in a coming major transformation of society, after which all things will be changed.)

One can liken this phase in one's life to a moral clumsiness, like a young creature trying out its legs for the first time. This desire to make a contribution is very appropriate and necessary, but unfortunately achieves ends that are some-what more parochial and less grand than fixing the world.

The actual purpose of this conscience becomes apparent when, with the collaboration of your hormones, you are seduced into a breeding liaison with a significant other. Marriage and, more so parenting, provide the first real experience of having to consider the needs and aspirations of another over your own.

At some point every spouse will experience the equivalent of the sage advice an old man gave me when I was young. 'Marriage, my boy,' he said, 'is not give and take. It's give and give'. We have indicated before that the degree to which you deal with another person on the basis of self-interest is the degree to which you are in conflict with that person. Because of the inescapable proximity of a spouse, the scale of that conflict in the context of marriage very quickly escalates to one of deeply disruptive proportions. Marriage, more than any other relationship, is one that is so intense that the conflict that self-interest produces becomes insupportable. Where your parents could not have changed you, your spouse will!

> ' Marriage, more than any other relationship, is one that is so intense that the conlict that self-interest produces becomes insupportable. '

The truth that you are here for the other becomes even more accentuated once you have children. No infant asks for permission to wake you up at 3am. It is not in the least concerned about the fact that you have had interrupted sleep for a month and that you really need a good night because you have a major presentation tomorrow. Infants have absolutely no doubt that your role is to make them happy and to make them happy now, irrespective of the cost to you. There is no experience quite like parenting that teaches you that you are here to serve, unconditionally.

We are dragged out of the narcissism of adolescence by the insight that we really cannot seek to be happy alone. If my happiness means your unhappiness then, in the fullness of time, you will make very sure that I become unhappy. To be happy we all have to be happy. We commit to marriages and close relationships because we understand that our own happiness lies in enabling the happiness of others. I can only be happy if I make everyone else happy.

The project of enabling the happiness of others is primarily a providing project. It is concerned with going to work to earn a living, to pay the mortgage and put the kids through school. If you asked married people why they go to work, for example, more often than not they would say it is to provide for their children.

You could confront them by saying that they are only at work to get things. They are fundamentally here for money, for purely self-serving motives. Should the person be honest they would admit to this, but they would say they are doing this to provide for their families. They are getting money from work to give; they get to give. In other words, they would articulate the Third Intent.

One can also describe the character of this epoch in our lives as generous, precisely because of the emphasis on provision. It is fundamentally about things. We feel a lot more disapproving of a parent who forces their child to suffer material want than we do about one who does not give of her time to a child. In the West, where the baby boomers produced the age of the Second Intent, their parents, the people who fought in WWII, produced the age of the Third Intent. Happiness was a Ford Prefect car with three round-faced kids on the back seat.

> 'The project of enabling the happiness of others is primarily a providing project. It is concerned with going to work to earn a living, to pay the mortgage and put the kids through school. '

The Third Intent is the epoch of duties or of knuckling un- der for the social good. It is about being the exemplary citizen. We spend a lot of time in this epoch – possibly twenty years or more. That is two decades dedicated to making everyone else happy; putting them through school and paying the bills. Providing and providing to the point of exhaustion.

And then, one fateful day, you wake up early in the morning. As you sit on the bed you look down at your legs and cannot help but notice the swollen feet, the varicose veins and the warts. You glance over the acreage of the large bed you have managed to acquire, at the significant other snoring on the other side, who has also become repulsively obese and has developed the most objectionable halitosis.

Your morose musings then turn to the three offspring you have brought forth in this liaison. The oldest is in Papua New Guinea with a bone through his nose. The second eldest, the one you never really liked, became an accountant like you.

The youngest whiles away his time alternating between lying on the coach watching TV and smoking cannabis in the back yard. Slowly, a deep sense of outrage starts to boil up within. You think to yourself: 'They said that I was not allowed to be happy on my own. I could only be happy if I made others happy. I have worked to make them happy. I have slaved away at a job I disliked, developed a dicky heart and a paunch and I am miserable. I have not discovered this happiness on the other end of a togetherness rainbow. I am more alienated than I think I have ever been'. The phenomenon is called a midlife crisis.

> 'The sense of rebellion that gives rise to a midlife crisis is entirely legitimate and understandable. It is true: you were told a lie.'

In our current culture, very few marriages survive the midlife crisis of either spouse. They have both worked so hard at their respective careers and on the provision project, that their lives have quietly and incrementally gravitated away from each other. They now feel that they have more in common with colleagues at work than with each other.

He joins a gym, grows a ponytail, buys a motorcycle and has an affair with his blond, 25-year-old secretary. His spouse goes to a Pilates class, among other things. One evening, she gets a bit drunk at a convention and has a fling with her boss. If you were to ask them how two such fine, upstanding citizens could misbehave so badly after years of marriage, they will both tell you the same thing: 'I have to get my life back!'

The sense of rebellion that gives rise to a midlife crisis is entirely legitimate and understandable. It is true: you were told a lie. You bought into the pretty picture of the Ford car and the chubby kids. You discover that there was no happiness for you there, that it was a ruse to get you recruited to the Great Procreative Project.

Aiming the outrage at the spouse, the kids or the job is not appropriate. If I base my happiness on that over which I have no control and then feel powerless and unhappy, surely the fault does not lie with the object of my aspiration. It lies with me for having based my happiness on such flimsy foundations. The appropriate response to a midlife crisis is not to rebel against the world; it is to examine the intent that has produced the unhappiness. The work of the latter part of life does not sit in the outward, with the other, no matter how beautiful and alluring. The work sits on the inside, with your intent. This insight produces the transition point to the Fourth Intent.

The Fourth Intent: I am Here to Give

The Fourth Intent commences with a deep personal crisis that can be understood as the dark night of the soul. It is a time when all aspirations appear futile and life itself is experienced as a bit of a cruel joke.

1st Intent	2nd Intent	3rd Intent	4th Intent
GREED	FEAR	GENEROSITY	COURAGE
I am here to get.	I give to get.	I get to give.	I am here to give.
All is Function.	Meaning is functional.	Function is meaningful.	All is meaning.

It is a time where one realises that although many of the aspirations that you thought would make you happy have been achieved, it is this same unhappy person who gets out of bed every morning. This experience enables the motivation to start doing the only work that really matters, the work of one's own intent.

What has happened prior to this point is that the self has learnt a principle of delaying gratification further and further to achieve the outcome of happiness and fulfilment. The overall process looked something like the following:

The child: 'I will scream until they give me what I want. I want happiness now.' Over time the other resists what the infant wants and the infant is frustrated by not getting what it wants. This enables a change: 'If I demand, they get angry with me, I have to be nice to them to get what I want. To be happy I have to get them to like me'.

The adolescent: 'If I am always nice to them they don't take me seriously. The issue is not to be liked; the issue is to be taken seriously. If I compete and win, then they will like me and I will be happy.'

The adult: 'If I compete to win, it means they have to lose. If they lose, then they no longer affirm me, they find me objectionable. My happiness cannot be based on their unhappiness. For me to be happy, I have to enable them to be happy. Then they will see me as significant.'

At each stage of development the point at which the moment of happiness arrives gets delayed further and further: I scream to get what I want now, I am nice to get something tomorrow, I compete to win at the end of the year and I serve them so that eventually, in the long term, (God knows when, a decade?) we will all be happy together. The end of the Third Intent and the beginning of the Fourth Intent is when the preposterousness of the idea of delaying gratification becomes painfully apparent.

Taking and Outcome, Giving and Process

The revolution in the architecture of intent commences when the self starts to experiment with a new possibility of the formulation of intent, one which has little to do with the end, the outcome, but has everything to do with process. The groundwork for this possibility is laid in the architecture of any moral act, of an act done with the intent to give.

I shall return briefly to the example of Fred and Joe that I referred to earlier:

Let's say I have two subordinates at work, one called Joe and another called Fred, and let's assume that I am very knowledgeable about something which they both have to do, because I had done it in 1980. If I say to Joe, 'In 1980 I did the work that you have to do now and the way I did it, worked. Don't argue with me, just do what I did.

	MEANS	ENDS	INTENT
JOE	PERSON	JOB	TAKE
FRED	JOB	PERSON	GIVE
	PERSON?	RESULT/JOB?	

But to Fred I say, 'In 1980 I did what you have to do, and it worked. You may find it helpful to take a look at it.'

When one examines the difference between the two interactions, a number of things become apparent: Firstly, it is clear that Joe could possibly find the interaction negating, while Fred will probably find the interaction more affirming. Secondly, Joe will experience my demeanour as autocratic because he is left with no choice and Fred, who has a choice, will experience my demeanour as democratic. On the surface, at least, the interaction with Fred conforms to all of our nice ideas of political correctness.

It becomes apparent that there is more going on than just the autocratic or democratic nature of my behaviour when you separate two variables in the interactions – means and ends – and put into those two categories either the person who is doing the job, or the result achieved by the job:

Clearly, in Joe's case, my intent is to get the job done and I am using Joe as my means or resource to get it done. In Fred's case, however, it is quite possible that we will have a different result from what I had in 1980. In fact, the result could well be a disaster. This means that my intent in this case is not to get a job done, it is to teach Fred something. I am using the job as means to enable Fred.

> ❛The Fourth Intent is about developing the understanding that the purpose of doing things, is to do them well – to commit to the process.❜

If one considers the difference between these two interactions from the point of view of intent, it will be clear that my intent in Joe's case is to get something out of him – to take. Whereas, in Fred's case, it is to give him something. In Joe's case, my intent is purely concerned with the outcome, so what is significant to me, and what is getting my attention, is that which will achieve an end in the future. In Fred's case, I am trying to be helpful to him; therefore, I am directing my attention to his requirement, and I am using the outcome as a means to achieve that purpose. In Joe's case, my attention is on the outcome, while in Fred's case, it is on him and the process itself. In Fred's case, my purpose is the process, or being correct with Fred. The Fourth Intent is about developing the understanding that the purpose of doing things, is to do them well – to commit to the process. In so far as there is an outcome, it becomes the means to achieve the purpose of doing things well. If I am walking, I do not walk to get to the destination; I use getting to the destination as an opportunity to have a good walk.

The shift of attention from outcome to process is consistent with the shift of intention from taking to giving. This means that I do not need to be doing things to achieve happiness as the outcome. I can be happy by basing my happiness on doing what I do well. I no longer base my happiness on an outcome, on what I am getting, but rather on the process of what I am doing or giving.

I will always be happy if I base my happiness on the quality of what I am giving, because that is always in my hands. This means that being happy is not the result or the output of action; it is the input. My intent is not an emptiness that seeks to be filled; it is a fullness that empties. Rather than acting to engineer the conditions that would make me happy, I am unconditionally happy and therefore I act.

The achievement of this happy state of affairs is rooted in surrendering all outcomes. It is about acting unconditionally in the very best interests of the other as it is presented in the moment that you are in. Because a person's conditional motive is based on their conditioning, the ability to act unconditionally requires escaping one's own conditioning. It quite literally means undoing who you have been made to be – to discover who you really are.

We come into the world as magical, scintillating point of awareness. Over time, we become increasingly confined. We think we are so old, have so many kids or have many preferences. We develop these convictions about who we are over time, and each one of them describes a limitation.

> ❛I will always be happy if I base my happiness on the quality of what I am giving, because that is always in my hands. This means that being happy is not the result or the output of action; it is the input. ❜

> **❝ I rediscover that I am that ecstatic, magical being who I was before I became deined. I am in the same state of connectedness that the infant experiences. ❞**

The web of these statements of limitation produces the architecture of our intent. My limitation describes my weakness, my lack. It therefore also provides the criteria for what will complement lack – what I need to be fulfilled.

When I forego that web, I rediscover that I am that ecstatic, magical being who I was before I became defined. I am in the same state of connectedness that the infant experiences, but the direction of my intent has inverted. It is no longer constructed on what comes to me or what I get; it is constructed on what leaves me or what I give.

The Fourth Intent and Courage

This ability to give unconditionally is really the preparation for the ultimate end of our lives, which is death itself. The grave is the final examination of our intent. It asks us only one question, which is, 'Are you able to give or lose every- thing unconditionally right now?' The purpose of the deconditioning of our intent is to enable us to face this terrifying prospect. One can therefore describe the Fourth Intent as an epoch of courage.

This courage is not solely concerned with the ability to die, it also about the capacity to be unutterably alone. Our ultimate destination is not the great convivial love-in that we pursued in the Third intent. It is the completely singular aloneness of the grave. Even if we should die together we would not turn it into a conversation point. 'Hey Angela, I can't breathe anymore, can you still wiggle your toes?'

The Fourth Intent is about re-acquainting ourselves with who we really are, that magical being who came into the world before it was made a person among people.

That being is a colossus; it is beyond limitation; it is free and wild. It has more in common with the stars than it has with men. The conversation which that being has is not just with his fellow men, it is with the universe. To that being all is meaning.

Chapter 5

THE PRACTICE OF CLARIFYING INTENT

Changing the Register of Internal Dialogue

O ur intent is carried in our internal dialogue. As we walk through the world, there is a continuous internal chatter going on that comments on everything we observe. It recalls past injuries and delights, and entertains hopes and fears about the future. This chatter spins a web of meanings that fuel our intent.

Our intent is not only animated by our explicit hopes and fears. It takes shape in every comment we make on the world. If you could record what was going on in my head as I walked down High Street, it may sound something like, 'Mm, nice pair of legs, is that child pretty, oh wow, look at the car. That old woman is ugly!' Another person walking down the same street may be saying something like 'Gee, nice dress, very nice weather today, oh, there is the train station, sweet old lady.'

One is tempted to ask if we had indeed walked down the same street. From one point of view we have not. What I noticed as I walked down the street was something very dif ferent from what the other person noticed. In fact, what we noticed says less about the street than it does about what is important to us – what our own intent is.

Not only is our intent carried in the bold and explicit thoughts that we consciously entertain, such as, 'Am I going to accept or reject that offer?' But it also lives in a morass of tangled bits of internal dialogue that jostle with each other, somewhat like the hubbub in a crowded convention centre.

Some of the elements of meaning in this hubbub are explicit, but most are whispered so quietly that they are almost imperceptible. Our internal dialogue is comprised of layers of meaning that, on the one hand, are clear and explicit and, on the other hand, plummet away into the depths of vague musings and impressions. Generally, the subtler these whisperings are the more profoundly they in fluence both our intent and our experience.

> ‘Generally, the subtler these whisperings are the more profoundly they inluence both our intent and our experience.’

Our internal dialogue produces what it feels like to be in our own skin. Our bodies do not distinguish between impressions that are imagined or actual. If, for example, the image of a snake is projected on the internal screen of my consciousness, my body reacts with the same fear as seeing it in the street.

Our bodies react with the appropriate chemical respons es that correspond to the meanings that are revolving in our internal dialogue. If we keep on musing about fearful things, our bodies will be fearful and our postures will be defensive. Being in our own skin will be an unpleasant experience. By contrast, if we reflect on pleasant things, our bodies will produce the chemicals associated with feeling good. We will feel robust and have open and expansive gestures.

What it feels like to be ourselves is a product of the register of our internal dialogue. If we are to grow, we need to acquire a key skill – the ability to change the character of our internal dialogue.

Journaling as a Diagnostic Tool

It is not possible to correct or repair something without a diagnosis. It is therefore important to develop some diagnostic skill with regard to one's intent. As we indicated before, for most of us, our intent is a mixed bag. We are somewhere along a continuum of grey in the mix of our intent. This complexity is presented to us in the hubbub of our internal dialogue, and because those elements of our internal dialogue that have the deepest influence on our intent are subtle and inexplicit, actually working out what our intent is, is often easier said than done.

As we indicated before, your internal dialogue produces what it feels like to be in your own skin. We know, for example, that if your intent is fundamentally here to take, you will be insecure, discontented, weak and in conflict with your world. By contrast, the degree to which your intent is to give unconditionally, is the degree to which you experience yourself as secure, fulfilled, powerful and in harmony with your world.

Keeping a journal is an ideal diagnostic tool. I suggest one starts with what we could call a 'what's-it-like-to-be-in- your-skin-omometer'. This instrument has four calibrations: Insecure-Secure, Discontented-Fulfilled, Weak-Powerful and Conflict-Harmony. The first use of a journal is to allow you to record, on a daily basis, how you feel regarding these calibrations, with a very short exploration as to why you think you feel that way.

To get maximum use out of the instrument it is important to build as many reflective steps as possible into the process of journaling. You can, for example, on a weekly basis, read the daily submissions for that week and then write a summary of the week. Every month, you would read the four weekly summaries, and then write a summary for the month. Every quarter, you would read the three monthly summaries for the quarter, and summarise the quarter, and every year, you would read the four quarterly summaries for the year, and write a summary for the year. The effect of doing this is to build a series of reflective steps that require you to pull away further and further from the minutiae of your day-to-day experience in order to get a more overall perspective on your life.

Journaling as a Remedial Tool: Transforming Resentment to Gratitude

When we examined the issue of transactional correctness, we concluded that just as gratitude sits at the core of the intent to give, so resentment sits at the core of the intent to take. It is as if there are fundamentally two perspectives or sets of lenses for viewing the world. When we view the world through the gratitude lenses, we are seeing things as they are, and the actions that flow from that are normally constructive and wholesome.

However, when we view the world through the resentment lenses, we are fundamentally doing violence to the truth and cannot trust anything we are subsequently going to do. Anything we do from the perspective of resentment entrenches our insecurity, discontentment, weakness and conflict with the world. We need to develop the key skill of being able to transmute resentment into gratitude.

The T-Exercise

The T-Exercise is designed to enable the shift of your experience from resentment to gratitude. It can be made part of a journaling practice, or it can be done separately as the need arises. The basis of the technique lies in the in- sight that our emotional response to what we experience in the world does not exist independently of the register of our description of the event. When we describe an event in terms that emphasise the loss, we feel insecure, discontented, weak and in conflict. When we describe the event in terms that frame it as a gain, we produce an experience of security, fulfilment, power and harmony.

The T-Exercise is so named because the instrument looks like a T. It requires one to provide three deliberate descriptions of an event that causes you resentment.

T-EXCERCISE	
THE FACTS	
THE WORST VIEW	**THE BEST VIEW**

The process is as follows:

1. Deliberately describe, as clinically as possible, what happened; sticking only to the facts and not allowing yourself any value judgements. The register of this description should be like an objective police report, without moral comment on what happened.

2. Deliberately look at the event from the worst possible point of view. In this step, you emphasise the harm and the hurt that came from the event, taking care, though, not to get unrealistic in the description. Because I twisted an ankle does not mean I am crippled for life.

3. Deliberately seek the blessing in the event. This may be challenging, but is possible if you do not allow yourself to indulge in any self-pity. No matter how bad a thing was, if it did not kill you, then by definition, it was not unbearable. This insight alone has a blessing in it, because it reminds us of our strength.

4. Once you have written all three accounts, pause for a while, allowing the implications of what you have written to sink in. The next step is to read the worst description and to highlight any words or phrases that resonate with the categories of malevolent intent (see diagram below). You then read the best description and underline any words or phrases that resonate with benevolent intent.

5. Now pause and reflect upon which of the two descriptions, the best or the worst, is true? Clearly they are both true. Because they are both true, it means that you are not doing violence to the truth by claiming the best description to be true for you.

TRANSACTIONAL CORRECTNESS The BENEVOLENT and *MALEVOLENT* Categories		
	REFLECTION	**ACTION**
ESSENCE	AWE *(Terror)*	SIGNIFICANCE *(Arrogance)*
ATTRIBUTE	SUBMISSION *(Rebellion)*	POWER *(Control)*
SECONDARY ELEMENT	TRUST *(Distrust)*	COURAGE *(Cowardice)*
PRIMARY ELEMENT	GRATITUDE *(Resentment)*	GENEROSITY *(Selishness)*
ROOT	SEEING THINGS AS THEY ARE *(Presumption)*	GIVING EACH SITUATION ITS DUE *(Expediency)*

What follows is an example of the instrument applied to a recent event on our property:

THE FACTS

There have been a number of thefts from our property over the last six months. Previ‐ ously, the wheels had been stolen from vehicles of people living on the property. This was normally discovered as people wanted to leave for work in the mornings. None of the thefts affected my own property. On Saturday one of the men living on the property named Rene, told me that he had noticed something suspicious at the gate. When we went to investigate we found that the motor of the gate was no longer there. It had been very carefully removed, with damage done to the motor mountings of the gate. We had a number of people coming to join us for a party that day, including the labourers from an alpaca farm. One of these labourers, a man called Junaid, told me that he knew the man who took the gate motor and suggested we go to ind him. I mentioned this to other men who were at the party, many of whom offered to help. In total eleven men went along on the expedition to recover the motor. When we got to the house of the man in question, he was not there. His wife said he had not been at home since the previous evening and, seeing that we did not believe her, she allowed us to look through the house. We found neither the man in question, nor the motor.

THE WORST VIEW

What happened last Saturday is atypi‐ cal example of the collapse of law and order in South Africa. After having suf‐ fered a number of thefts on our prop‐ erty, it was inally our turn. Rene told me there was something wrong with the gate and when we went to investi‐ gate we discovered that some bastard had stolen the motor. Everybody who came to the party agreed that nothing was safe in the country any more and agreed that we feel helpless. It's use‐ less to take a case like this to the police and I knew I had lost the motor. Junaid said he knew who took the motor and eleven men came with me to ind the thief. When we got to his house, he was not there and, after looking through the place, we could ind no trace of him or the motor. The escapade was a total waste of time.

THE BEST VIEW

The response of my friends to the is sue last Saturday was really gratifying Rene bothered to come and tell me that the gate motor had been sto len, despite the fact that it was not his property Junaid was quite willing to point out the thief at considerable risk to himself He lives in the area and could be identiied by the thief after wards. I felt deeply supported by my friends, eleven of whom were quite willing to go out of their way and help in the matter. When we arrived at the man's house, they all conducted themselves admirably There was no shouting or threats of violence from any of them. Although we did not re‐ cover the property, the experience made me feel like I am not alone, that people do look out for you despite what people say about South Africa.

When applied to this account, it becomes apparent that while both the best and worst descriptions are perfectly valid, how I feel about the event will differ greatly depending on which of the two descriptions I choose to make the truth for me. The T-Exercise is therefore a method to quite deliberately exercise the distinction between the proverbial half-full or half-empty glass and to choose to make the half-full glass your truth.

The T-Exercise Applied to Guilt

We have just explored how important it is to transmute resentment into gratitude and indicated how the T-Exercise is a method that enables that shift. We normally reserve the idea of resentment for the other. I am resentful towards him or her for having done X or Y.

However, we do something similar with ourselves when we feel guilty. Both guilt and resentment keep us trapped in an unresolved drama, which continues to reproduce the blood chemistry of ill feeling within ourselves. Having worked with these ideas throughout the world, I have become aware that there are indeed very large variations in how people view the issue of guilt. In some contexts, it is viewed as important to contain the damage of your wrongdoing. Thus, confessing to your spouse about your affair is not viewed as a particularly virtuous thing to do. Elsewhere the view may be quite different. In some contexts, the issue of making reparation is seen.

> Both guilt and resentment keep us trapped in an unresolved drama, which continues to reproduce the blood chemistry of ill feeling within ourselves.

Both guilt and resentment keep us trapped in an unresolved drama, which continues to reproduce the blood chemistry of ill feeling within ourselves, to be critical. In others, there is an acceptance of the role of the courts to define reparation.

While I do not presume to make a call on the merits of these various approaches, it does seem to me that there is a blessing to be found even in my own misbehaviour if, for no other reason than I now know that I don't want to go there again. We often cycle in a pattern of misbehaviour precisely because we do not own up to the fact that we have done it.

Metaphorically, we look away rather than at the event, because looking at it is just too unpleasant.

Should I view the event as blessing, however, I would be less inclined to look away from it and be more comfortable to learn from it. The T-Exercise is a very good tool to apply to this end, but I suggest you apply it to the self in this instance, and not to the other.

Petty Tyrants

The T-Exercise is a very useful tool to deal with things that happened in the past. I have, however, been challenged on its usefulness in ongoing issues, particularly when concerned with difficult relationships or people. We all have that one person in our lives who drives us to distraction, and very often that person has real authority over us or at least has the capacity to instantly make us miserable. In these instances, I have found the idea of the petty tyrant to be very helpful.

The petty tyrant is device used by Carlos Castaneda to make the most annoying people in your life your allies in the pursuit of achieving your highest development as a person. Although the following Sufi story is not from Castaneda, it indicates very eloquently what petty tyrants are about:

A Sufi shaykh was once approached by a student who was complaining bitterly about his wife.

'Oh shaykh!' the man exclaimed, 'this woman I am married to is an awful person! Last week my mother came to visit and this good for nothing wife would not make her tea! The other day she refused to cook my supper, but instead threw the food on the floor in a fit of rage! And just yesterday...'

The shaykh listened for a while and then snapped at the student. 'Shut up!'

'Why?' asked the student.

'Look,' the shaykh replied, 'your relationship with your spouse is like the relationship between a vessel and the water it carries. It is the nature of water to find where the cracks in the vessel are. It is poor courtesy of the vessel to complain when the water finds the cracks.'

When people do things to us that we experience as annoying, our annoyance indicates more about our own conditional motive than it says about the inherent nature of the other person's behaviour.

Nothing demonstrates this more profoundly than the extreme irritation we experience at the annoying habits of people from other cultures. I was brought up to eat with my mouth closed and never to speak with a mouth full of food. I have worked among people who exhibited a complete disregard of this basic courtesy, something that I experienced as indescribably challenging.

On the other hand, I am convinced that I did things that they found outrageous. I remember scandalising colleagues in Thailand once by pitching up at a wedding dressed in black. It's regarded as an unlucky colour. What this indicates is that our annoyance with people says infinitely more about our own conditional motive and our own conditioning than it says about the other person.

There is a hidden treasure to be found in our annoyance. We have said that the process of our maturation is concerned with the maturation of our intent. We described this maturation as an incremental foregoing of our conditional motive, and thus an incremental deconditioning of the self.

The most profound device to scout the lay of the land of your intent is a petty tyrant.

> **'A petty tyrant gives you the firsthand experience that indicates to you what your conditioning and your conditional motives are. '**

A petty tyrant gives you the firsthand experience that indicates to you what your conditioning and your conditional motives are. If you sincerely wish to escape your conditioning, find yourself a petty ty- rant if you don't already have one. Serve this person unconditionally in a spirit of great generosity and courage. Transmute your resentment toward them into gratitude, because by their misbehaviour, they offer you an invaluable gymnasium to work on your own intent.

The petty tyrant really comes into its own as a journaling technique. It gives you the means to sincerely shift the register of your appraisal of an impossible person from resentment to gratitude. It is an incomparably useful tool, one of the very many devices for which we owe Carlos

Castaneda a vast debt of gratitude. What I have described here is a most basic and crude use of the device. It can be used far more elegantly, but in order to explore how to do that, I recommend you read the man yourself.

Forgoing Manipulation: Treating People as People and not as Things

Your frustration with people provides a very useful tool to reflect on the degree to which you view people as people or as resources for the pursuit of your own ends. Fundamentally, being here to give has to mean that it is inadmissible to treat another human being as your instrument. When you are here to give to people, you do not use them as the means to your end.

Nothing shows up our manipulative ruses more than the resistance we encounter from people when we seek to manipulate and control them. It therefore stands to reason that when you experience resistance from someone, it is useful to consider what you want from this person that is causing the resistance.

When we find ourselves trapped in a cycle of internal dialogue that is concerned with justifying ourselves, it is a sure sign that we have got ourselves hooked in a manipulating drama. The more we seek to demonstrate that we are right and they are wrong, the more we need to ask ourselves why we are so hell-bent on justifying ourselves.

The need to justify is a confession of a kind. It is an expression of guilt because, at some level, you have been the tyrant. The resentment that you experience toward the petty tyrants of your life has a similarly unpleasant feel to it. Again, it does not matter whether we are dealing with guilt or resentment; they both light the way for us to transcend our conditional motive. Your daily journal is the surgical table for both these cancers. It provides the context for you to be able to take what is inside you and put it outside you, so that you can gain some perspective on it.

Establishing a Value Set

The final thing that I find useful in a journalling process aimed at changing the register of our internal dialogue, is developing an explicitly defined value set. When we reflect on whether what we have done or intend to do is right, it puts us in a good position to face our own manipulative ruses. I would like to refer to the criteria against which we make this judgement as a value set.

However, for a value set to be useful to us in this way, we need to be quite deliberate about how we define a value. Firstly, I think it is crucial to differentiate between a need and a value. Just because something is important to you does not mean that you can call it a value.

> '*The need to justify is a confession of a kind. It is an expression of guilt because, at some level, you have been the tyrant.*'

> 'Just because something is important to you does not mean that you can call it a value. '

I may have an irrepressible need to pocket goods at a store without paying for them. This does not make theft a value. I remember being scandalised by a lefty friend of mine at university who had a part-time job at a bookstore. He thought it was quite legitimate for him to steal books from his employer because he was poor and he wanted them, and his employer was a dirty capitalist.

What we have indicated so far about being here to give, is that it is not just about being nice; it is about acting with generosity and courage. It was necessary to deal with the issue at a slightly more pragmatic level because otherwise the issue of giving remains too abstract. It would seem to suggest that being here to give is not about always being nice, an assertion that would be both impractical and untrue.

Just as the idea of being here to give is possibly too abstract, one could also view the distinction between generosity and courage as too broad to be practically useful.

Say, for example, that you meet a woman whose husband has just been killed in a car crash. No one else knows this has happened; you are the only person who knows the man has passed away. What is the appropriate thing to do? Whenever I present people with this scenario, the overwhelming majority will answer that you should tell her that her husband is dead. When I ask them why, they most often indicate that it would be dishonest not to tell her. If you are privy to information that will affect someone else, it seems dishonest not to tell them.

If one considers this example from the point of view of the distinction between generosity and courage, it is immediately apparent that the quality you would require to tell the woman about her husband, is courage. This is not an easy conversation to have. However, this is not the same kind of courage as beating up the thug in the park who is mugging the little old lady. You would not slap the unfortunate wom an about as you were telling her that her husband was dead. This suggests that to be courageous does not always require confrontation. And, similarly, being generous does not always mean being nice. One can speak very appropriately about the generosity of the surgeon's knife. This indicates that there is a level of abstraction missing between the level of generosity or courage, and the level of behaviour, of what you are actually going to do. We refer to that as the level of values.

This level does not have to be populated with a plethora of elements. Around seven elements would suffice, such as honesty, fairness, respect and so on. In defining the value set, it is important that one does not only require a sin- gle word or phrase for a value. One should also give some thought to what acting consistently with the value actually means behaviourally. This value set is yet another mirror; a tool you can use in your daily journal.

TRANSACTIONAL CORRECTNESS The BENEVOLENT and MALEVOLENT Categories		
	REFLECTION	**ACTION**
ESSENCE	AWE (Terror)	SIGNIFICANCE (Arrogance)
ATTRIBUTE	SUBMISSION (Rebellion)	POWER (Control)
SECONDARY ELEMENT	TRUST (Distrust)	COURAGE (Cowardice)
PRIMARY ELEMENT	GRATITUDE (Resentment)	GENEROSITY (Selfishness)
ROOT	SEEING THINGS AS THEY ARE (Presumption)	GIVING EACH SITUATION ITS DUE (Expediency)

TRANSACTIONAL CORRECTNESS The BENEVOLENT and MALEVOLENT Categories		
	REFLECTION	**ACTION**
ESSENCE	AWE (Terror)	SIGNIFICANCE (Arrogance)
ATTRIBUTE	SUBMISSION (Rebellion)	POWER (Control)
SECONDARY ELEMENT	TRUST (Distrust)	COURAGE (Cowardice)
PRIMARY ELEMENT	GRATITUDE (Resentment)	GENEROSITY (Selfishness)
ROOT	SEEING THINGS AS THEY ARE (Presumption)	GIVING EACH SITUATION ITS DUE (Expediency)

Chapter 6

THE EIGHT ATTENTIONS

U p to this point, we have been exploring the process of maturation through the lens of intent. The key contention being that at birth the infant is here to get nconditionally and at death the individual gives or loses nconditionally. We concluded that the process of maturation is concerned with the process of the maturation of the intent to give nconditionally.

On reflection, it becomes apparent that intent is really concerned with how we engage time. If we asked someone, 'What do you intend to do?' the answer would more than likely refer to something in the future. 'Why are you digging the furrow, Aslam?' 'So that I can lay a cable.' 'Why are you mixing the flour and the water, Susan?' 'So that I can make pancakes.' The answer to the question refers to an outcome.

This is also true for activities done now with regard to something that took place in the past. 'Why are you building the wall?' 'There are barbarians in the forest.' 'Why are you shooting the horse?' 'It has gone lame.'

Although the motive behind the activity refers to something that has happened in the past, the intent of the activity is to produce an outcome. Outcomes are time-based. They happen at the end. Therefore, intent is concerned with how we engage time. This makes the issue of intent very useful for a first exploration of the issue of maturity, because it produces an eloquently simple, linear discourse. It is informed by one dimension pinned between a single set of binary opposites: beginning and ending; birth and death.

There is a linear character to how we conceive of and deal with time. It is a line that moves from the past, through the present, to the future.

However, as in all things, the strength of this perspective is also its weakness. It is precisely the simplicity of the perspective that produces its limitations.

These limitations become apparent when you examine the latter end of the process of maturation.

When you consider the Fourth Intent, for example, it becomes clear that the moral register of the idea of the intent to give breaks down in the face of a completely unconditional act. Being here to give unconditionally has to mean doing what is appropriate, irrespective of outcomes. We argued that from the point of view of the Fourth Intent, the measure of a man is not his achievements; it is what he does when catastrophic failure is a foregone conclusion. Because the word intent wants an outcome, we find it difficult not to see the idea of the intent to give outside of the intent to produce benign outcomes for others. In fact, the language of intent sits uncomfortably with anything done truly unconditionally. 'Why are you walking up the mountain?' 'To walk up the mountain.' 'Why are you driving through the traffic?' 'To drive through the traffic.' 'Why are you sitting in the dining room?' 'To sit in the dining room.' One can almost hear an audible 'Huh?'

> 'The measure of a man is not his achievements; it is what he does when catastrophic failure is a foregone conclusion.'

If one wants to deal with truly autotelic intent, in other words, intent that disavows any interest in an outcome, one needs a framework that is a bit more sophisticated than a simple, time-based discourse.

> ❛Intention is concerned with why we do what we do. It is concerned with action. Attention is concerned with what we see. It is concerned with perception.❜

That framework is concerned with attention, rather than intention. It is immediately clear that these two discourses will relate, because what is important to you, what your intent is based on, will translate into what you give attention to. In this sense, intention and attention are intimately related issues.

Our normal experience of things is framed in two variables, time and place. If you had a time but not a place, it would be difficult to understand how you could 'be'. Similarly, if you had a place but not a time, it would be safe to say that you 'are not'.

We have already seen that the faculty whereby the self engages time is intent. The faculty whereby the self engages place is attention. Intent is concerned with how we deal with now. Attention is concerned with how we engage here. Intention is concerned with why we do what we do. It is concerned with action. Attention is concerned with what we see. It is concerned with perception.

Attention

There is a clear relationship between what is important to us, what we see, and why we act. A man walking through a landscape is, metaphorically speaking, swimming through a soup of sense perceptions if he does not distinguish between what is significant and what is insignificant.

It is this distinction between what is significant and insignificant that produces boundaries. It delineates objects and allows them to stand out from their surroundings so that they can be perceived as separate objects. This suggests that no two people can ever walk through the same landscape.

Let's consider, for example, two significantly different people walking through the African bush – a hunter and a tourist. As he walks through the bush, the hunter will notice fine nuances that will help him to spot game. He will read a story in the twist of a blade of grass, a bruised leaf or a broken twig. Indeed, these things will stand out for him like neon lights. His attention will pick out these and other things, while the intensity of the midday heat or the sharp- ness of the sunlight will be part of an insignificant background to what he perceives.

The tourist, on the other hand, will have a very different experience. He could be admiring the vastness of the African bush, while squinting and suffering under the bright midday sun. These will be overwhelming foreground experiences, and the subtle nuances that the hunter would pick up, are entirely lost on him.

These two people are effectively walking through two different landscapes. What the one person sees as significant and there- fore, pulls into relief, the other person sees as quite insignificant. One can go as far as to say that it is fundamentally meaningless to speak of the landscape as an independent 'objective' reality.

Each of the two landscapes observed is a perfectly legitimate rendition of the truth.

They both refer to the same collection of sensory stimuli. They differ in what the perceiver regards as significant or insignificant. What the hunter sees as significant is abstracted from the surrounding body of impressions and produces what he sees as the landscape. Exactly the same is true for the tourist, and in so doing, he produces a very different landscape.

> 'No two people can ever walk through the same landscape. ... What the one person sees as significant and therefore, pulls into relief, the other person sees as quite insignificant. '

> ❛The difference between what is significant and insignificant is rooted in the intent of a person. ❜

The difference between what is significant and insignificant is rooted in the intent of a person. What you want to achieve will clearly set the criteria against which things will either be significant or dismissed. In this sense, a person's intent acts like a filter, it produces the criteria against which things are pulled into the foreground. In other words, they are seen as significant, or pushed to the background to join the mo rass of other sense perceptions that are not worthy of notice. It is very important to note that without this happening, one cannot properly speak of perception.

Without the intent to find distinction, everything perceived will be camouflaged to blend with everything else. Not to perceive difference is to not perceive. That difference may be nuanced and allow large areas of ambiguity. If all things seen are seen as the same, it is the same as being blind. It means to not see at all.

The Perceiver and the Perceived, The Inward and the Outward

The binary opposites, if strictly defined, that intent is rooted in, is the distinction between beginning and end, birth and death. The primary binary opposites that attention is rooted in, is the distinction between the perceiver and the perceived. The most elegant way of describing this distinction is to examine how vision works. If you focus on a point directly in front of you, you will notice that everything you see is contained within what we can describe as a boundary at the limit of your peripheral vision.

INWARD ——————————————— OUTWARD

If you turn your head to look at something else, what you will be focusing on will still be in the centre of what you see, and the rest of what you see will still be encapsulated by this boundary at the limit of your peripheral vision. This boundary therefore acts like a frame – a window frame – containing everything you see. It is for this reason that we refer to everything that is contained within this boundary as the window of perception. The window of perception produces a boundary between two radically different worlds. In the first instance, there is the world itself – that which is perceived. This world is seen as contained within the window of perception and is presented in front of it. It is therefore appropriate to refer to that which is contained within the window of perception as the outward.

It is on that side, the other side of the window of perception. On this side of the window of perception is the perceiver – the self, the observer, the one who is doing the looking or perceiving. Because the perceiver is on this side of the window of perception, it is appropriate to refer to the realm behind the window of perception as the inward.

The outward is that which is contained by the window of perception and includes all sense perceptions. The inward operates behind the window of perception. The distinction between the inward and the outward is the key distinction on which attention is based.

The Significant and the Insignificant

Attention is a much more complex issue than intent. Intent presents us with clean lines and a simple, linear discourse pinned between a single set of binary opposites.

SIGNIFICANT

INWARD   OUTWARD

INSIGNIFICANT

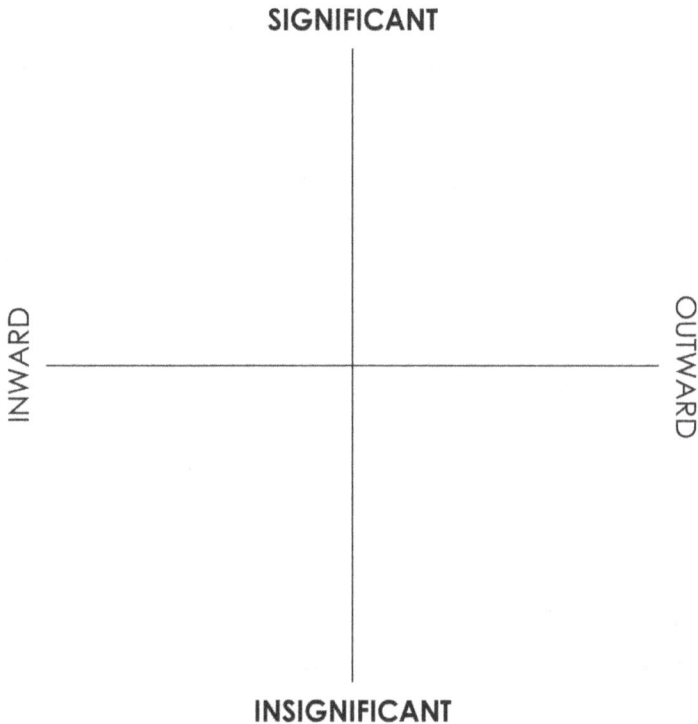

Attention, on the other hand, is concerned with the interaction of two sets of binary opposites: the distinction between the inward and the outward, and the distinction between the significant and the insignificant. Another way of understanding this is to say that the distinction between the outward and the inward makes no sense if, simultaneously, there is no distinction between the significant and the insignificant. How can there be any differ ence between the experiencer and the experienced if the experienced itself is not differentiated? If all perception becomes indistinguishable soup, the perceiver will necessarily be part of the broth.

For attention to arise, there are necessarily two sets of binary conditions: the inward/outward distinction and the significant/insignificant distinction. Of these two sets, the difference between inward and outward has to be primary. Sequentially, there has to be a perceiver before there can be perception. So the very first distinction on which all other distinctions are based, is the difference between the inward and the outward. The first meaningful perception is that there is an observer here and an observed there, and it is this perception which forms the root of all other perceptions. An investigation of attention is an investigation into how things appear. Hence it becomes apparent that this will include two issues: The first is actually how things stand out to be perceived, that is, the mechanisms that afford things significance. How, in the moment, they are apparent and differentiated from the soup of all experience; or stay unapparent and part of that soup. As we have already established, the criteria by which things assume significance are rooted in the intent of the observer. The second issue is how things seem to be – how they appear to be, as opposed to how they are.

How Things Seem to Be

When examining perception, it is important to recognise three implications of how things seem or appear to be, which follow on each other in a logical sequence.

Firstly, for things to appear at all seems to require the insignificance of the observer or the inward. Our eyes most usefully demonstrate how attention works. They are designed to look at anything other than ourselves.

This suggests that our attention is made for the other. It is made to be fascinated and enamored with the other. As soon as we make ourselves the object of our fascination, we become deeply disturbing, like a person whose eyes have rolled back into their head. The other (the seen, the outward) is that which appears to be significant. And the seer (the self, the inward) appears insignificant. Just as the eye which sees itself is blind, so too is the I.

> **'Just as the eye which sees itself is blind, so too is the I.'**

The second implication of how things appear to be, follows on the first: For perception really to happen, significance has to be granted to the observed – the outward. The observer, or the inward, therefore initially appears to be subordinate to the seen. This experience that the inward appears to be subordinate, and the outward appears to be superordinate, is the most constant experience that the observer has to contend with. In the first instance, if I try to locate the outward, that which is not me, I find it encapsulating me. The other stretches away from me, into infinity, in every direction from me. It presents it- self as overwhelmingly vast and I, by contrast, appear to be puny. I find myself to be an insignificant speck encapsulated by phenomena of galactic proportions.

I am encapsulated by the other not only in space, but also in time. The very first perception that I would have been aware of, would have been of other than me. The first time I opened my eyes to see, it would have appeared to me that what I opened my eyes on, was already there. In that sense, it would have preceded me. It is my alpha.

> **' The other, the observed, is my alpha and my omega. The inward appears to be subordinate to the outward in both space and time. ,**

I imagine that when I die, there will, at some point, be a last impression. I will see something in my window of perception that will still be there after the window closes. In this sense other than me would follow me, it would succeed me. It is my omega. The other, the observed, is my alpha and my omega. The inward appears to be subordinate to the outward in both space and time.

The third implication of how things appear to be, follows from the second, which is that the observer, the inward, is subordinate. This subordinate status of my attention is not a sense of an impersonal sub- ordination to cold and galactic events. It is a status which also requires an intensely personal and individual fostering by the outward, by that which is other and significant. The light of my attention does not operate independently of the body in which it is housed. My body provides a scaffold on which the light of my attention finds footing to shine out on the world.

When I look down at this body, it becomes immediately apparent that there is a magnificent sense of design to it. I have not created my hand with its opposing thumb and fingers or my amazing digestive system that can transform a vast array of fuels into my ability to act and observe. My attention is sustained by an incalculable number of metabolic events that I personally cannot account for. The scaffold of my body has been bequeathed to me, rent free, until I die.

> ' I am the product of a fine weaving together of all events since the Big Bang. '

Not only has other than me preceded me, it has done so in a way that has produced me. I am the product of a fine weaving together of all events since the Big Bang. The possibility for me to be, has been bequeathed to me by other than me. Other than me therefore not only appears as superordinate, it is also that which nurtures.

Not only does it nurture, but by the very fact that I have not produced the function of the mechanism that produces me, so too I cannot account for its dysfunction. It is unlikely that I will die by my own hand. This means that the dysfunction that will eventually kill me, will be visited on me by other than me. However, even if I should die by my own hand, it remains true that the finger that pulls the trigger does not account for the fact that a disrupted brain equals death. As other than me has brought me here, so too will it remove me. My engagement with it is not an impersonal engagement with unconscious mechanical processes. It is a deeply personal connection in which it is the custodial lord, and I am its product, its slave. To adequately account for attention, therefore, one cannot merely refer to the distinction between the significant and the insignificant. One also has to account for how things appear, or seem to be. It appears that attention is uniquely individual, and that both the significant and the insignificant have a deeply personal and individual character. They stand in relation to each other where the outward appears to be the significant, superordinate lord, and the inward appears to be the insignificant subordinate slave.

Gatheredness: The Inwardness of the Insignificant

Behind the window of perception lies the realm in which all experience is gathered. If one considers this visually, the limit of my peripheral vision forms a boundary that contains all I see. This limit extends from the corners of my eyes, away from me, to meet the furthest horizon I see.

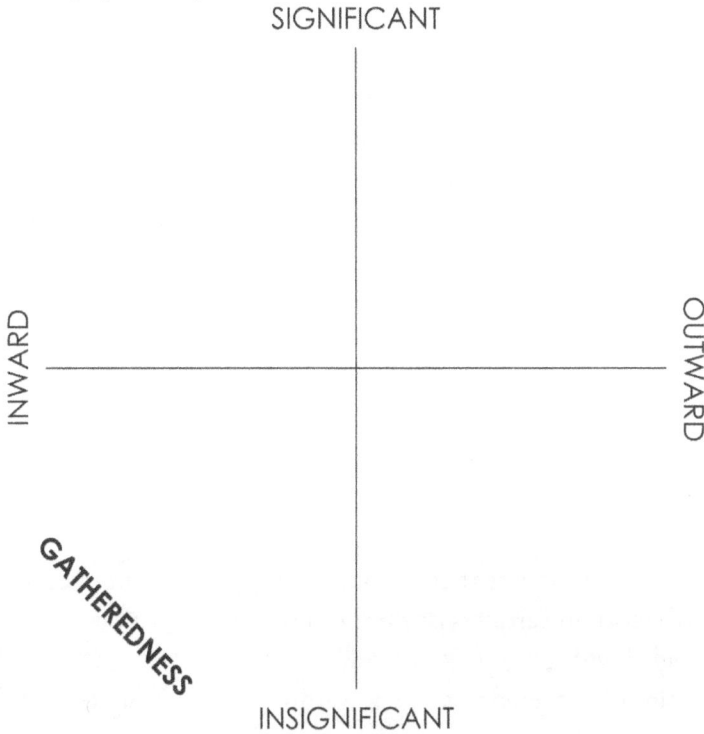

SIGNIFICANT

INWARD

OUTWARD

GATHEREDNESS

INSIGNIFICANT

For perception to happen, everything contained between the furthest horizon and the limit of my peripheral vision is gathered into the intensely private realm of the perceiver, of the inward. It is therefore appropriate to describe the inward as the place of 'gatheredness'.

This place of gatheredness is a place of unassailable intimacy, a place that can never actually be invaded and occupied. Just like you can never get behind someone else's eyes to see their world, so too nobody can ever get behind yours. They may have a good idea of what is presented in your window of perception because they asked you, or had some other way of interrogating your experience, but your experience remains your experience. It is permanently and fundamentally inaccessible to another. It is yours, uniquely and most intimately yours.

The realm of gatheredness is the place of secrets and is expected to be so. Our socialisation demands that we put a filter on our mouths. You cannot just blurt out the first thing that comes to mind. You have to show restraint. You have to guard your engagement with the world so that only that which is basically benign and constructive to the other gets out. For anyone to claim that the possibility of doing something quite shocking never occurred to them, would clearly be dis- ingenuous. One cannot judge the person for having had the shocking thought, but you can judge them for the shocking act.

The inwardness of the slave is the place of intimacy. In an intimate relationship one can and should show forbearance. You are intimate with someone to the degree to which you accommodate their incongruities. Intimacy implies that. This suggests that our inwardness is where our own incongruities are lived with and struggled with.

> ‘This place of gatheredness is a place of unassailable intimacy, a place that can never actually be invaded and occupied. ’

The realm of gatheredness, the inwardness of the insignificant, has no form. It is, rather, a vessel in which forms occur. It is a dark spaciousness that contains thoughts, memories, images, sense impressions and feelings. Although it is a most intimate realm, it is a place that is rarely deliberately navigated. It is what most people refer to when they use the term ‘myself’. There is a dizzying complexity to this realm. It contains much that is most often even beyond the grasp of the perceiver. It is a container of immeasurable depth, where most of its contents lie hidden in a dark, fathomless abyss.

Separation: The Outwardness of the Significant

The outwardness of the significant is the great world as it appears, out there. It is the place where things stand out to be perceived and are granted significance. For something to be significant, everything else that is not that thing, has to be insignificant. This realm is therefore a realm where things are separated, where they stand out to be perceived. It is the realm of separation.

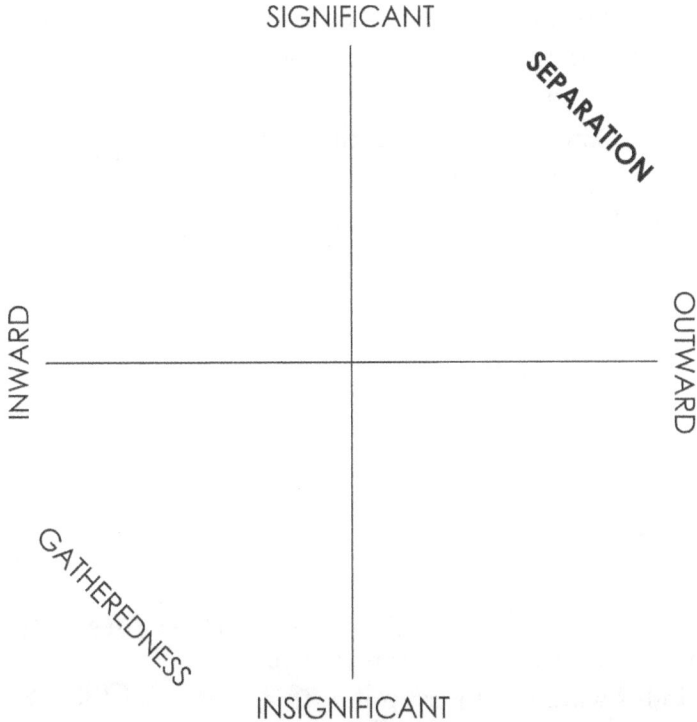

SIGNIFICANT

SEPARATION

INWARD

OUTWARD

GATHEREDNESS

INSIGNIFICANT

Separation presents itself as the binary opposite of gatheredness. Where gatheredness is a realm of intimacy, separation is a realm of alienation. It is the realm where things stand apart, are separated. It is also the realm where things contend. For the one thing to appear, or stand out, every- thing else has to be negated or sup- pressed. Separation is a realm that is constituted of elevation and abasement, domination and subordination, the big and the small. It can also be described as the realm of the majestic – the realm of the stars, mountains and vast phenomena.

When compared to the form of the perceiver, that vast- ness is deeply abnegating. The perceiver is experienced as immeasurably small, whereas the perceived is immeasurably huge. The perceiver is vulnerable and the perceived unassailable. While the perceiver is transient, the perceived was already there when the first perception happened and will continue to be there once the perceiver passes. The perceiver appears finite whilst the totality of the perceived appears to be infinite.

Form: The Outward of the Insignificant

The outwardness of the insignificant is that part of the perceiver that is presented to him in his window of perception. It is the perceiver's form. As I sit writing this, I do not experience myself as a disembodied spirit. There are things that I perceive in my window of perception that are clearly objects like other objects, yet are somehow connected to my in-

While the perceiver is transient, the perceived was already there when the first perception happened and will continue to be there once the perceiver passes.

As I type this, I notice my hands. They are objects like any other, yet immediately respond to intentions that are being formulated behind my eyes, in the inward.

From this point of view, there are two kinds of objects that are presented to my window of perception. There are objects that are clearly of the other, but there is also a class of objects associated with the self, the perceiver.

> **'** While the perceiver is transient, the perceived was already there when the first perception happened and will continue to be there once the perceiver passes. **,**

The objects that are associated with the perceiver collectively form the boundary between the perceiver and the perceived. When I look down at my body, what I see delineates me from the rest of th world, from the other. It is the shape that my inwardness operates behind. It is something that I can see, but which is also seen by others.

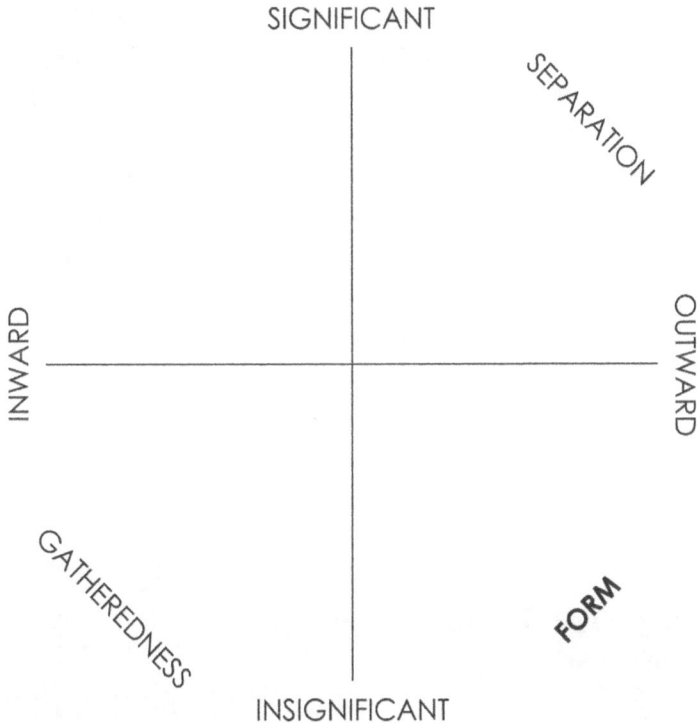

SIGNIFICANT

SEPARATION

INWARD

OUTWARD

GATHEREDNESS

FORM

INSIGNIFICANT

This realm is a border realm. It is a realm which is both me and not me. It is the realm that enables my intercourse with the world and with which the other interacts. The realm of form is also the realm of the insignificance of the outward. Anything that appears in the outward does so by virtue of its form. Its form is the delineation of its boundaries. The boundary of a thing also describes its limitation. The boundary separates the thing from what is not the thing. No matter how great the phenomenon, what is not the phenomenon will always loom majestically over it.

Everything we concluded about the apparent insignificance of the inward are also true for any particular outward phenomenon. There was a time, for example, when the bear was not. Then, the appropriate environment, the copulation of its parents and the succouring embrace of its mother's womb all intersected to produce the bear. What was not the bear preceded the bear and gave rise to the bear. What was not the bear was the bear's alpha. Throughout its life the bear was sustained by what was not the bear. The food, air and water that sustained the bear, that informed the bear, was bequeathed by other than the bear. The bear was not only sustained by what other than the bear bequeathed, but also by what other than the bear withheld. The hunter did not find the bear. The falling tree trunk missed it. And then one day the bear was stalked by a hunter. The hunter took aim, fired his rifle and then the bear was no more. The bear's body decomposed and returned to the earth.

The bear came from what was not the bear; it was sustained from other than itself; it was protected by other than itself; it was destroyed by other than itself, and it returned to other than itself. In what way, then, can we assume the mighty bear to be anything but subordinate and insignificant?

Exactly the same has to be true for anything that appears in the outward, from the most majestic to the most insignificant. The significance of any given phenomenon is a borrowed robe. Its very form designates its insignificance.

Meaning: The Inwardness of the Significant

Hidden in the inward there is a realm that denotes significance. When the perceiver becomes aware of this realm, he is introduced to a truly spectacular insight. Nothing in the outward is significant without me designating it as such.

This suggests that although the inward appears insignificant, it is only apparently so. The outward is the realm of the majestic, of the king. The inward is the realm where what is majestic is defined, where the king is made. Who then, has greater significance, the king or the king maker?

> 'Nothing in the outward is significant without me designating it as such.. Who then, has greater significance, the king or the king maker?'

SIGNIFICANT

MEANING

SEPARATION

INWARD

OUTWARD

GATHEREDNESS

FORM

INSIGNIFICANT

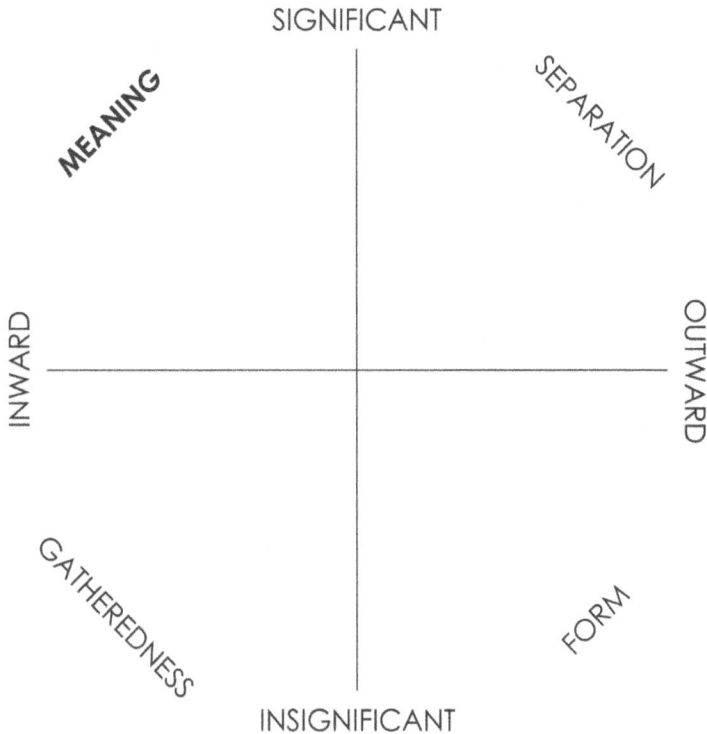

The outward is the realm where forms appear, the inward is the realm where significance and meaning are defined. It is this definition which grants that which appears its boundary, its form.

Things are for me by the meaning I ascribe to them. I have absolute autonomy to define that meaning. Where someone may be terrified of snakes, I may choose to love them. Where another may have a mortal fear of heights, I might relish them. Where someone else may perceive a contending foe, I may choose to perceive an ally. And this clearly has nothing to do with some 'objective' truth.

Losing a limb in a battle objectively seems to denote my frailty and vulnerability to the overwhelming forces of the outward. Yet, I could choose to see this event as a gymnasium that tempers my spirit and teaches me fortitude. By my own authority I designate the catastrophe and the blessing, and the foe becomes the ally.

The capacity to designate meaning makes the perceiver truly autonomous and authoritative; king-like. The significance of the inward is the capacity of the inward to confer significance and meaning. The realms of form and meaning are therefore binary opposites. The realm of meaning is also the realm of intent.

The Maturation of Attention

We have already observed that attention can only produce a perception by distinguishing between the significant and the insignificant. Attention is drawn towards what is significant, and away from what is insignificant. This simultaneous attraction-repulsion action produces a sense of imbalance. Any imbalance is simultaneously a move toward something and away from something. This imbalance produces the engine for the maturation of attention.

As attention matures, it progresses through eight epochs which we will refer to as the Eight Attentions. Each Attention has a principal quality that would describe the overall character of how attention operates in that epoch.

However, these Attentions are dynamic, because they also contain within them an imbalance, a simultaneous move toward, and away from, two extremes of a binary opposite. Over time, the imbalance inherent in a given Attention overcomes the inertia of that Attention and there is a fundamental shift in how attention operates. This shift delivers at tention to a new, more mature station.

> 'Attention is drawn towards what is significant, and away from what is insignificant.'

Because intent and attention are so intimately related, there are very useful parallels to be drawn between the Four Intents and the Eight Attentions. Generally, the First Intent relates to the First and Second Attentions, the Second Intent relates to the Third and Fourth Attentions, the Third Intent relates to the Fifth and Sixth Attentions, and the Fourth Intent relates to the Seventh and Eighth Attentions.

Examining maturation through the lens of the Four Intents is particularly helpful for the immature epochs of one's life. However, the Eight Attentions are far more useful in examining the latter end of maturation.

The First Attention: The Insignificant

At birth, the infant is nine months away from not being at all. It has barely begun to appear. It is outwardly insignificant – still a speck of a being. It is clearly difficult to speak with much authority regarding its inward state.

Very few people can recall the first few hours of life, and it is impossible to interrogate the infant regarding its subjective experience. We are therefore left with a speculative reconstruction of the inwardness of the infant by examining them from without.

As we indicated before, at birth the infant seems to experience a fundamental continuity between the self and the other, or the inward and the outward. The reason for this is that there is very little mediation required to fulfill a need. All the infant has to do is grunt and her attending mother rushes to the rescue. Self and other, self and mother, are therefore perceived to be the same.

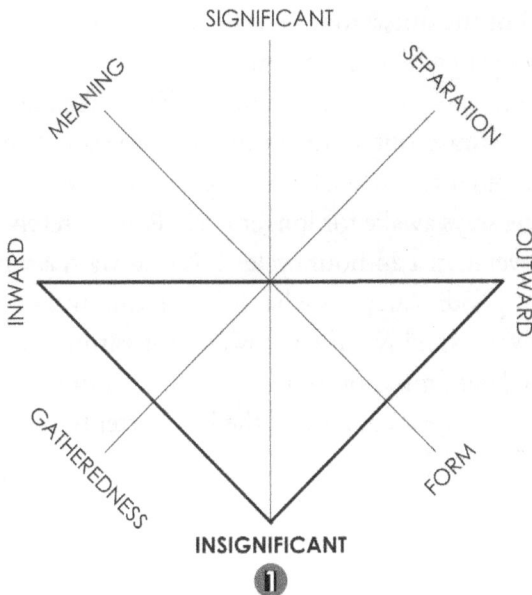

SIGNIFICANT

MEANING

SEPARATION

INWARD

OUTWARD

GATHEREDNESS

FORM

INSIGNIFICANT

①

The lack of separation between the inward and the outward must then produce a sense that all experience is indistinguishable soup. The infant is bathed in an ecstatic continuity of warm sense impressions which only start to be differentiated when some unpleasantness is experienced.

The lack of separation between self and other also produces an inability to distinguish significance in the outward. At best an infant at birth may be able to identify its own mother, but that is probably as far as the deliberate identification of significance goes.

It is inconceivable that the infant will know that the pink ball with hair on the chin is daddy and the brown one is Fluffy, the dog. They are all objects in the soup. Because the perceiver, the infant, has no form, no form is recognised, not even in the world.

> **Because the perceiver, the infant, has no form, no form is recognised, not even in the world.**

This First Attention is initially pinned between the inward and the outward. The infant rapidly oscillates between states of wakeful- ness and sleep.

In sleep she withdraws back into the inky depths of unconscious inwardness. When awake, her attention is captured by the intriguing stuff of the outward: the rattle in the crib; Fluffy's yelp when she tugs his ear.

This Attention has an imbalance, though. The imbalance is constituted of an attraction toward outwardness and a move away from inwardness. Very soon the rapid interchange between periods of sleep and wakefulness slows down. She stays awake for longer periods at a stretch. Furthermore, she sleeps less overall in a 24-hour cycle. The out- ward is where the action is; it's where the goodies are; it is what is interesting and significant.

This move away from inwardness toward outwardness eventually shifts the fundamental configuration of her attention from that of an infant to that of the crawler. The imbalance of the First Attention has delivered our heroine to the Second Attention.

The Second Attention: Form

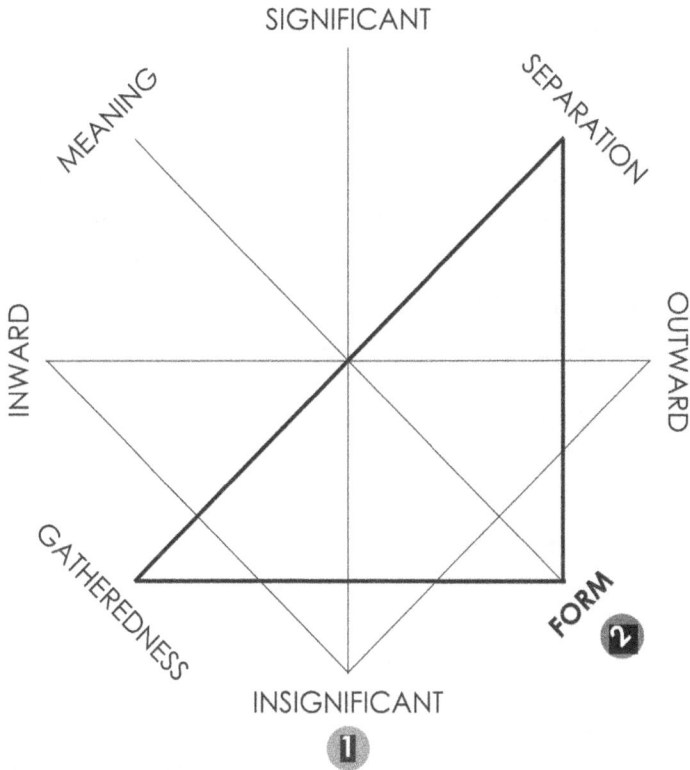

In the Second Attention, the attention is dedicated to the endeavour of appearing. It is as if the attention of the crawler is trying to push against the window of percep tion to see what the form of the subject is. It is a time of a fascination with mirrors, with dis- covering that you also have an outside; that you have a form.

Kitchen and grocery cupboards are particularly interesting at this stage of our lives. They provide a wonderful opportunity to bang things together – not just to see what things do when you bang them together, but also to see what you can do when you bang things together.

It is a thrilling exploration of the mechanisms that connect you with the world: your hands, your feet, your skin. And delight upon delight when you discover a packet of flour! The pure pleasure of breaking it open and pouring the contents over your head. The fascinating transformation it brings to your skin, which allows you really to see your own edges. Every adventure, both the pleasurable and the painful, not only teaches the crawler about the world, but also about herself: her shape, her boundaries and her limitations.

The Attention of Form is pinned between the binary opposites of gatheredness and separation. The crawler on the bus demonstrates this beautifully. He cannot wait to get off his mother's lap. He squirms to get on the floor and explore. He pushes away from the gatheredness of the intimacy of the lap to pursue separation. He wants to take shape. He wants to explore, to leave, to move beyond.

So she lets him. She puts him in the aisle of the bus, and he is off like a shot, as fast as his little hands and knees will take him, until he gets to the really scary old man in the flat cap who glowers at him from under his bushy eyebrows. Suddenly, our hero has lost all his courage and races back to the gatheredness of mother's lap, where he will sit, thumb in mouth, until the urge to explore again becomes irresistible.

In the Second Attention, we oscillate between gatheredness and separation, until the aspiration to separate becomes irresistible, and we are delivered into the wonderful world of the pre-adolescent child, the Third Attention.

> **'In the Second Attention, we oscillate between gatheredness and separation, until the aspiration to separate becomes irresistible.'**

The Third Attention: The Outward

In the Attention of the Outward, all our attention is concerned with exploring the world, the outward; and the inward is at best, a place of unconsciousness, and at worst, a place of night terrors. Where the Second Attention was all about exploring the outward form of the self, the Third Attention is about exploring the world. It is a time for running in the woods, for building kites and for dissecting frogs, not out of a sadistic perversity, but out of pure curiosity.

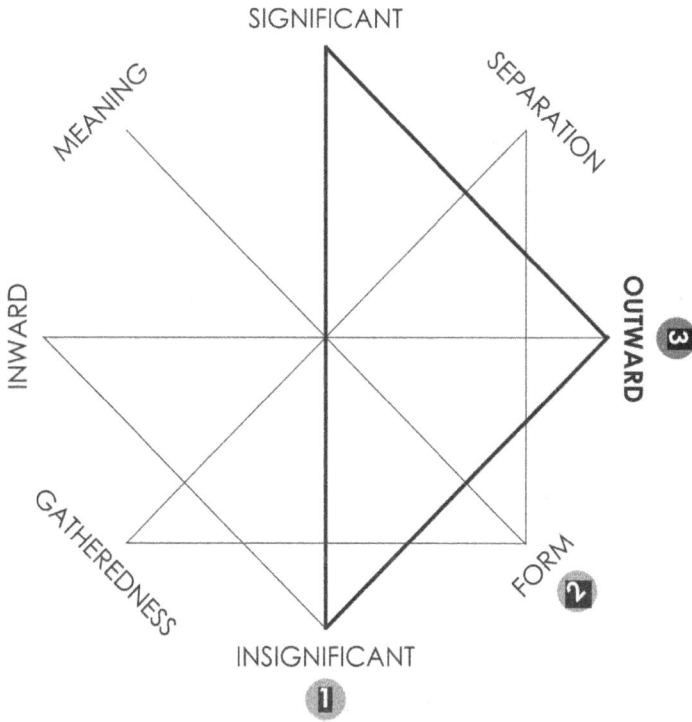

If they have not been dam- aged, children at this age are born naturalists. They love to keep living things, they love to run and explore. Seven-year-old Raees wakes up at six in the morning and is out of the house like a shot, collecting his mates to play. He comes home at dusk, exhausted and filthy. His mother lets him shower, puts some food in his mouth and gets him to bed, where he sleeps the sleep of the dead until the next morning, when he repeats the cycle. He keeps a box of scorpions under his bed, has a collection of WWII model aircraft and is a crack shot with a BB pellet gun. Shelley loves walking in the veld with her dad. They catch butterflies and, when no-one is looking, she climbs the gum- tree in the back yard. On Saturdays, she gets to groom the horses at the local stable. Life is a huge adventure. Life in this Attention is pinned between the significant and the insignificant. It is an attention of play. We act like we are doing serious, significant things, but they are not re- ally significant, and we know it.

We are not doing things for real; we are playing. Raees puts on his Batman cape and beats up the criminal rose- bush. He is being the big man setting things right. Shelley changes the nappy of her doll as gently as if she was a real mother, except she is not; she is playing. They are both playing an insignificant game of emulating the seemingly significant things that grownups do.

A further implication of being pinned between insignificance and significance, is that in this phase of their lives, children are busy finding their place in hierarchies. Again, unless they are damaged, pre-adolescent children are not fundamentally rebellious. They do not want to get rid of or replace the significant ones in their lives; they want their protection. Only after I had my own children did it become apparent to me just how much horror a child has at the prospect of losing a parent. For a pre-adolescent, this is truly too ghastly a fate to contemplate.

At the same time, they are very aware when they are superior to someone else. One of the less attractive aspects of this phase of our lives is that we become obsequious to bullies, yet very easily take a delight in bullying those weaker than ourselves.

As we indicated before, no Attention is static. In the Third Attention, the tension between significance and insignificance has a pull, or a bias, to significance, and a pull away from insignificance. Everybody wants to grow up and become big. This tension eventually unseats the Attention and delivers the self into full-blown adolescence.

> '**We act like we are doing serious, significant things, but they are not really significant, and we know it. We are not doing things for real; we are playing.** '

The Fourth Attention: Separation

I like to think of adolescence as a medical condition, part ly because my own was so challenging, but also because I have lived through the adolescence of others.

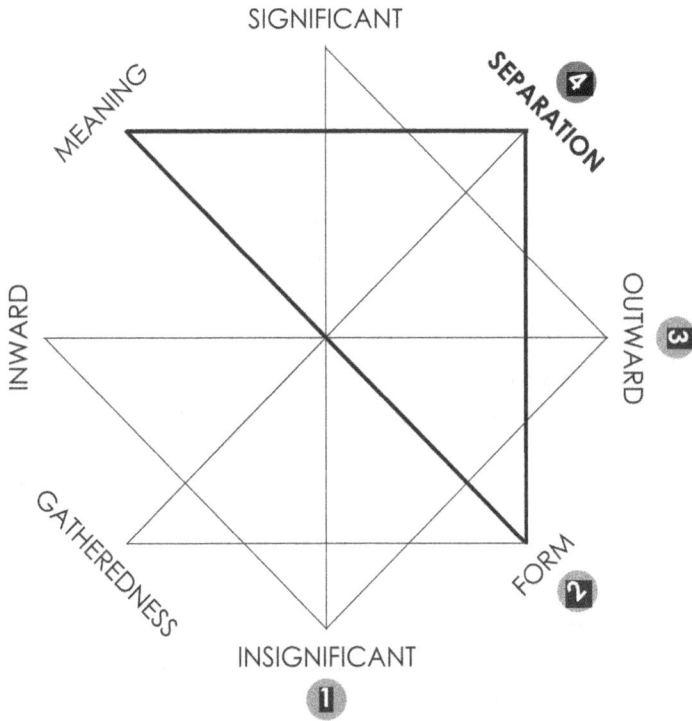

SIGNIFICANT

MEANING

SEPARATION 4

INWARD

OUTWARD 3

GATHEREDNESS

FORM 2

INSIGNIFICANT 1

The essence of the Attention is the aspiration to stand out, to be noticed, to be separate. This need to stand out translates into an intense competitiveness with others. It is as if the core programme is, 'I am separate from you; I am more significant than you'. Inter- actions with others very easily become win/lose interactions, eliciting storms of conflict and ill feeling.

The Attention of Separation is the time in our lives where we most intensely seek to manifest ourselves outwardly. It is an Attention which is concerned with standing out and being seen and admired. This intent to be seen is experienced as narcissism by others, which is why others, especially adults, find adolescents so objectionable. The reason for this is that a narcissist does something particularly ugly with their attention.

A useful metaphor to understand attention, is to consider how our eyes function, because our eyes are the most prominent organs that we associate with attention. My eyes are designed to look outward, at the other. This suggests that my attention has been made to be enamored with, fascinated by and enchanted with the other, not the self. Should I seek to make my own form a subject of fascination and enchantment, it is the equivalent of rolling my eyes into the back of my head. Because others find this distasteful, I should not be surprised that most engagements I have with others have an undertone of rejection, which entrenches my sense of alienation. In fact, for most people this Fourth Attention is the most miserable and alienated period of their lives.

The Attention of Separation is pinned between the binary opposites of meaning and form. Hence, one of the uncomfortable aspects of this Attention is the adolescent's struggle with authenticity. In the name of the battle cry, 'I have got to be me,' there is, however, a constant struggle to look like any other adolescent. The inner equivalent of the outer conflict that the adolescent suffers, is a deep conflict for authenticity.

It is this conflict that informs the adolescent's rejection of mere convention. Suffering the conflict of the inauthenticity of appearances, they want what is real, what has true meaning.

The counter culture of the 1960s was a manifestation of just this phenomenon. The skewing of the population demographics to adolescents in the sixties was the result of the post-war baby boom. This created the demographic condition where the conflicts of the adolescent could take on scale that mani fested in a social movement. The sixties in the West was the age of the adolescent.

In the growing of their hair, the smoking of pot and their promiscuity, what they really were saying to their parents was 'We reject your convention. We want what is real. We will go to the opposite ends of the earth, we will sit at the feet of the Maharishi Mahesh Yogi, but we will not have your ersatz superficiality. We don't want plastic, we want real. We don't want form, we want meaning.'

> 'Suffering the conflict of the inauthenticity of appearances, they want what is real, what has true meaning.'

It is precisely this struggle for the real and meaningful which, paradoxically, landed them in real jobs with real families and real responsibilities, in other words, landed them in the position of being the custodians of convention. They became the Baby Boomers. From being the self-styled custodians of Love, Freedom and Justice they became conventional adults. Sigh.

The Fifth Attention: The Significant

It is a sad fact of life that all our spontaneous good intentions are not sustainable if they are not institutionalised. In late adolescence the youthful commitment to big truths like Love or Justice or Freedom brings about a real requirement to col- laborate rather than compete with others. The self realises that being happy on my own is not an option.

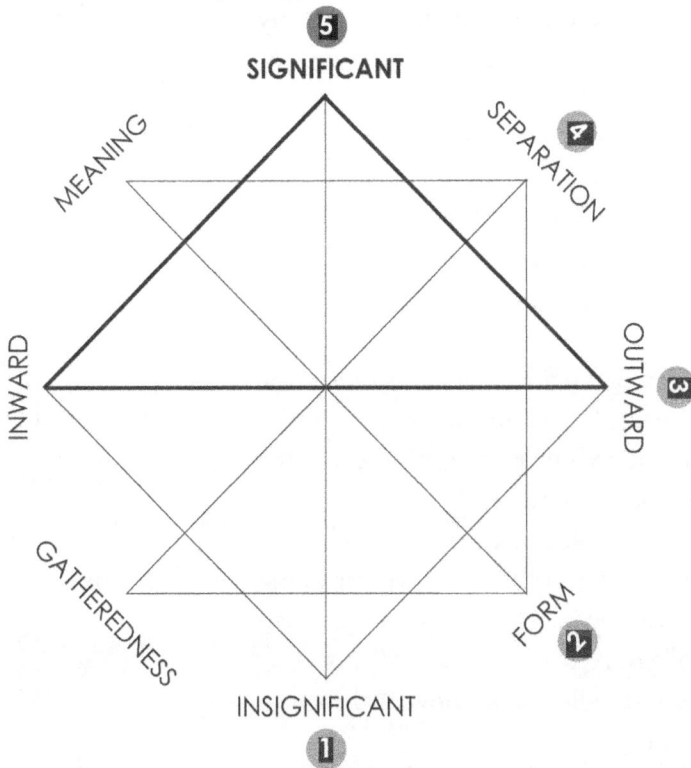

I can only be happy if that includes the happiness of others. There is the birth of a sense of responsibility that mutes the fundamental narcissism of adolescence.

This requirement for adults to collaborate is hard-wired into our condition. Our women gestate for nine months. Our young remain fundamentally in- capable of fending for themselves for a very long time.

We cannot repro-duce as a species if we do not collaborate. It is a village that raises a child. The condition that most profoundly describes the Fifth Attention is parenting. There is a natural alliance between the Fifth Attention and the First Attention. It is as if people in the Fifth Attention have been made for people in the First.

So in the interest of the pursuit of what is Good and Right, we are conscripted to being custodians of the village. We become duty and rule bound. Our first thought is not for our- selves; it is for our children. This is why married men do not make particularly good soldiers. They lack the recklessness of the adolescent.

I am reminded of an account of a killing of a man in the 1980s in the course of a factional dispute among Zulus in the district of Msinga. During a clash in a forest, two combatants from the opposing sides were separated from the rest, and ended up in hand to hand combat. After some time, one of the men was wounded and fell to the ground. His opponent sat on him, putting his spear to the wounded man's throat.

'Please don't kill me,' the man pleaded.

'I am not going to kill you now; I am going to wait until my brothers come, so they can see me kill you.'

'Please don't kill me, not now or then.'

'Why not?'

'I have children. Who will provide for my sons?'

'This morning, when you went to the corner in your house where you keep your weapons, why did you think you were coming here? Did you come here to talk? Did you think that only we would die and not you? Did you think of your sons then?'

This debate carried on for some time until the brothers came, and the wounded man was killed. What I found most moving about this account

> 'In the interest of the pursuit of what is Good and Right, we are conscripted to being custodians of the village. We become duty and rule bound. Our first thought is not for ourselves; it is for our children. '

was not that the man who was killed was a coward, it is very likely that he was not. However, he was quite prepared to face the humiliation of being taken for one, for the sake of his children.

> ❛We get exasperated at the hooligan adolescents for doing the very non-conformist things we did ourselves as adolescents. We become the stern commanders of what is right and forbidders of what is wrong. ❜

In the Fifth Attention, our impetuosity gets tempered for the good of others. We try to subscribe to convention. If we live in a culture that prizes interpersonal courtesy, we will be courteous. If we are in a culture that prizes a firm hand and good eye contact, we will cultivate a firm hand and good eye contact. We will do what we need to do because we need the help of others to live up to our own responsibilities. We need to conform.

Not only do we cultivate the courtesies that are the accepted conventions of our culture; we also propagate them in others. We get exasperated at the hooligan adolescents for doing the very non-conformist things we did ourselves as adolescents. We become the stern commanders of what is right and for-bidders of what is wrong.

This is particularly true in the early stage of our sojourn in the Fifth Attention. Of all siblings born to a family, one should wish to be the last born. The poor first-born child has the disadvantage of having parents who real-ly would like to do everything by the book. As young adults, we are least tolerant of deviation in others. We are extremely concerned with getting things right and doing things right. When we have our first child, he or she is most likely to be parented in a far more rigorous and bruising way than any subsequent children we may have.

The Fifth Attention is the Attention of the Significant be-cause it requires the self to embody the key characteristics that the community finds significant. The community places emphasis on qualities that will enable the individual to execute a custodial charge over the affairs of the community. This capacity to render custodial service to the group is true for every adult. Every adult, no matter how menial their position, has an implied deep custodial responsibility, for no better reason than the fact that they are capable of breeding.

In a sane society, the more a person is seen to be able to live up to their custodial responsibility, the more significant they are seen to be. Harry is less significant because he can only look after himself. Mark is more significant because not only does he look after himself, but he looks after the whole department. Jamie is most significant because he looks after the entire business.

The Fifth Attention is pinned between the binary opposites of the Inward and the Out- ward. This suggests that in executing their custodial charge, the person in this Attention is really trying to establish some form of balance between the needs of the self, the Inward, and the needs of the other, the Out- ward. With the passage of time, there is less and less of an insistence that things should be outwardly correct. There is a greater tolerance of ambiguity that comes with maturity.

This tolerance of ambiguity also means that the person allows themselves more leeway. Actually, it is not always necessary to do things just right. One can occasionally just do what is required to have a reasonable day. This growing calmness is also manifest in a decreasing interest in significance. The person is heading toward the end of their career and passes up the last promotion. Or in a corporate setting, the comment is made of the person that they are not hungry enough for the job; they are too close to retirement. Being the significant man is clearly no longer what floats the person's boat – but

> ❛ With the passage of time, there is less and less of an insistence that things should be outwardly correct. There is a greater tolerance of ambiguity that comes with maturity. ❜

being quietly contented does. There is a move toward inwardness and a move from outwardness.

The Sixth Attention: Meaning

In the Sixth Attention, there is the birth of the insight that happiness is to be found on the inside. There is the under- standing that you cannot always get what you want, and if you base your happiness on what you want to get, it will never be enough.

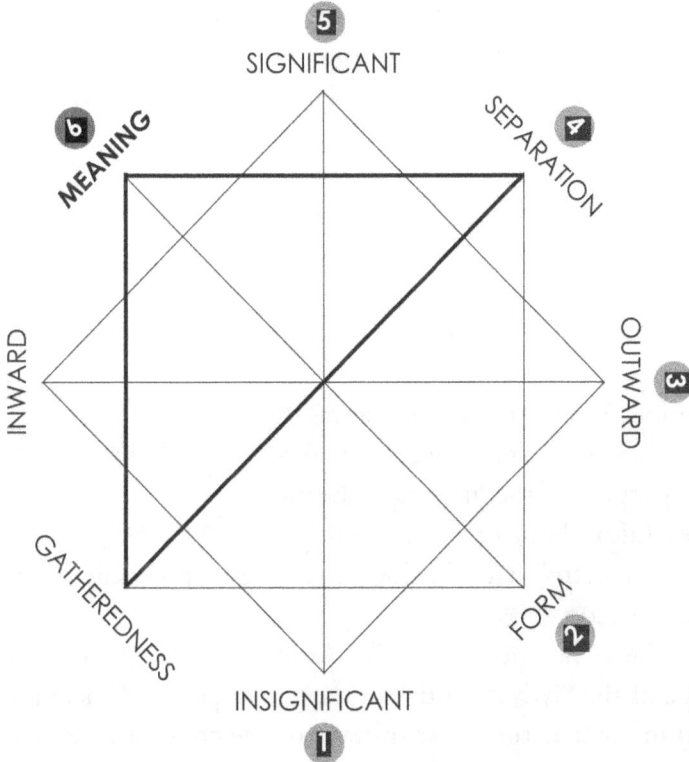

If you are unhappy, no amount of money or fame will change that condition. People in the Sixth Attention have lived long enough to have worked this out.

You have also lived long enough to work out that you decide the significance of what happens to you.

You have the life experience toknowthat you can choose for the glass to be half full. No matter how negative an experience is, you choose whether you are going to see it as a blessing or a curse. It is the designation of the thing as a blessing or a curse that produces the significance of the experience, not the experience itself.

People in the station of Meaning start to see things as they are, rather than how they appear to be. It may appear as if the inward, the self, is subordinate and the outward, the other, is the superordinate. In fact, this is not the case. Nothing I experience of the outward exists independently of the meaning which I ascribe to it. It does not define me, I define it. I am not its slave, I am its master. This mastery is not an explicit, outward mastery, though. It is the mastery of king-maker, rath er than of the king, and is far more profound than the mastery of the king, precisely be- cause of its subtlety.

The fundamental endeavour of the Sixth Attention is the pursuit of gratitude and appreciation. Where the cup of tea was the garnish of the important meeting before, now the purpose of the meeting is the nice cup of tea. Life is about a pleasant evening on the verandah, a stroll with the dogs and, delight upon delight, a morning with the grandson.

> ' Nothing I experience of the outward exists independently of the meaning which I ascribe to it. It does not define me, I define it. I am not its slave, I am its master. '

Where the archetype of the Fifth Attention is the young parent, the archetype of the Sixth Attention is the grand- parent. Where the parent will still insist that the sugar in- take of the child must be regulated, the grandparent sneaks a secret stash of sweeties to the child. The grandparent's interaction with the child is far less about the correction and edification of the child than it is about just appreciating the child. There is a natural alliance between people in the Sixth Attention and people in the Second Attention. Nothing brings more delight to a grandparent than a toddler.

The Sixth Attention is pinned between the binary opposites of Separation and Gatheredness, with a bias away from separation, toward gatheredness. Being the significant one who stands out is really not that interesting anymore. In fact, it is experienced as downright dangerous. People in this Attention know that to stand out means to become a target. They are far more comfortable with the small intimacies of day-to-day life. They have a predilection for the experience of gatheredness.

This predilection for gatheredness also gives rise to a growing interest in reflective pursuits. The person spends more time in prayer. They learn to meditate. They begin to see that inner work is perfectly legitimate work, in fact, more so than anything one can do in the world. They are about to embark on the journey to the final frontier, the only journey that really matters; the journey to the real Eldorado that all human beings carry in their hearts.

The Seventh Attention: The Inward

The attention of the Inward is really a way-station. It is the interspace where there is a fundamental inversion of how attention operates. Up to this point, the experience of the self was still that the self was encapsulated by the totality of the other. However, this idea is partly based on an illusion, and the illusion is that the self is an object like other objects. In the Second Attention, the observer sought to be known. There was an initial pushing of aspiration against the window of perception so that the self appeared more and more as an object in the world. This pursuit was refined and maintained through all the Attentions, reaching a zenith in the Fourth Attention and then gradually softening, with an increasing insight into the significance of the inward.

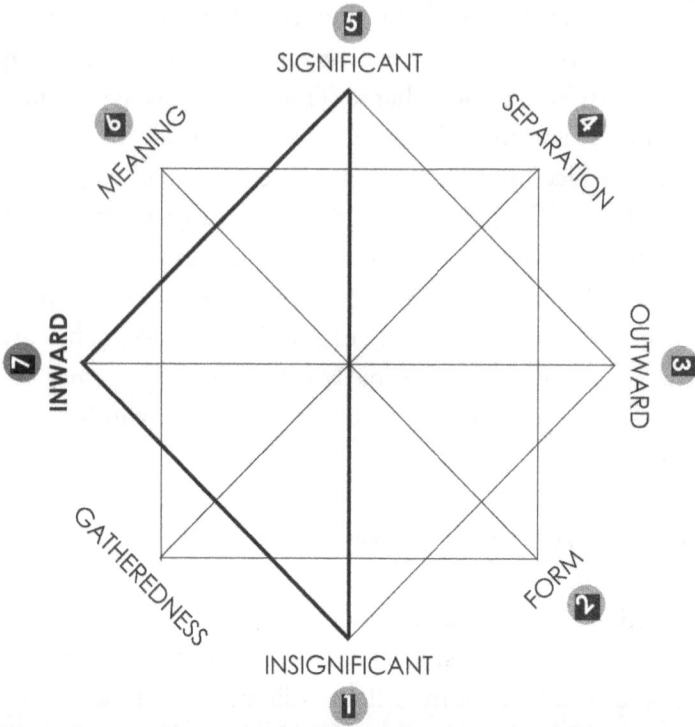

By the Seventh Attention, all endeavour is dedicated to inner accomplishment. To a normal person looking at this person from the outside, they would appear inscrutable. How do you come to grips with someone who has forgone all interest in the outward? It is possible that such a person would appear quite insane, or at least patho logically disconnected and disinterested.

This state is not pathological. It amounts to an heroic effort to withdraw all attention invested in maintaining the illusion that the self exists as an object. The process of objectification which commenced in the Second Attention is deliberately reversed. Clearly, the question is, to what end? As we said before, we are very used to thinking of the self as encapsulated by the totality of the other. In order to maintain this view, we have to allow the self to operate as an object. I can only see myself as surrounded by everything else if I stand in an imaginary third-person place, looking back at myself. Then I can see an object surrounded by other objects. This would then create the view that the self is encapsulated by the totality of the other.

However, this idea that the self is encapsulated by the totality of the other does violence to how perception actually works. I can never perceive what is behind me. Everything that I perceive gets presented to me in my window of perception, which is always in front of me. It may be that the source of the perception arises behind me, like a sound. But it still remains true that I experience the stimulus as there, whereas I am here. It is outside, I am inside, and the inside is behind the outside. All perception gets presented in the front of the window of perception.

If I try to investigate what sits behind the window of perception, I am presented with a spacious, dark emptiness that plummets away into a fathomless abyss. The Seventh Attention is concerned with dedicating all available attention to finding out what lies in the depths of that abyss. There is a complete dedication to moving from being significant to being insignificant. The consequent withdrawal of all attention dedicated to maintaining an outward persona creates the condition where the outward persona implodes. In all in ner traditions this phenomenon is referred to as dying before you die. It produces the Eighth Attention.

The Eighth Attention: Gatheredness

In the Eighth Attention, the self has forgone the illusion of existing as an object. The very boundaries that have been set up to delineate the self are gone, which means that the self no longer exists separately from the world. The original experience of ecstatic connectedness with all things that was experienced in infancy, is recaptured. All things are gathered to the inward, and the inward is gathered to all things.

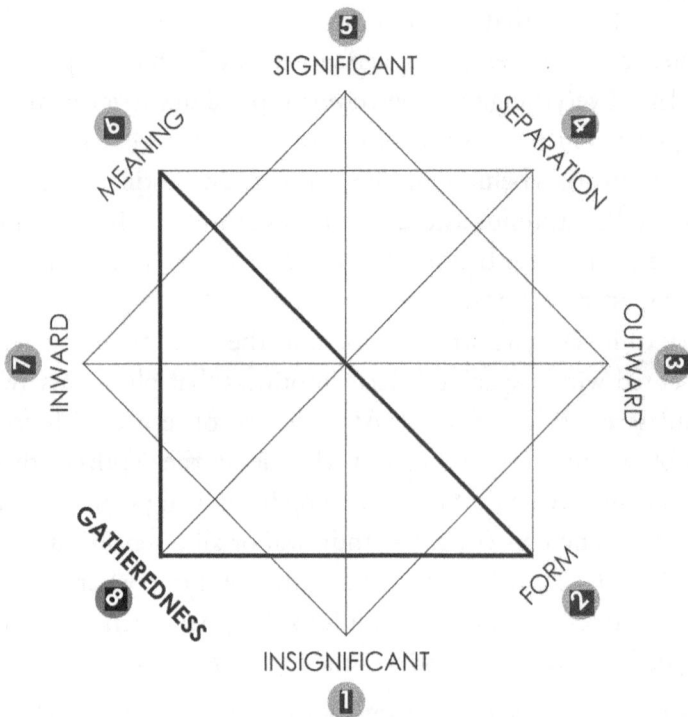

There is, however, a difference between this state and the state of the infant, in that this state is about being conscious of the nature of the inward. The single-minded dedication of attention to investigating what sits behind the in- ward drew the observer out of the world of objects. When such an observer then observes the world, the first insight is that all things perceived are presented in the window of perception, and that the inward is a dark spaciousness from which the perceiver operates. When the perceiver sinks back into that spacious- ness, it becomes apparent that the window of perception is not a flat, two-dimensional thing. When considered visually, it extends from the corners of my eyes in a circular sweep that ends at the furthest horizon. I am therefore, not looking into a flat plane; I am looking into a bubble. We can refer to this bubble as the bubble of perception, and all things that I perceive are presented to me in this bubble.

If I try to feel (with my consciousness or awareness) what sits immediately behind the point of observation, I find a vast emptiness. That emptiness, the inward, is the place from where the observer operates. If I felt what sits below the point of observation, I would find the same emptiness. If I felt above it, I would find the same emptiness. In fact, I would discover that the emptiness which is the inward, sits on the other side of the bubble of perception. The world does not surround me; I surround the world. I am not in the world; the world is in me.

> ❝The world does not surround me; I surround the world. I am not in the world; the world is in me. ... The totality of the self, the totality of my self, encapsulates the other. I am not the microcosm. I am the macrocosm. ❞

I would then know that I have been socialised into a view that the self is encapsulated by the totality of the other. I would know this to be false. I would know that the totality of the self, the totality of my self, encapsulates the other. I am not the microcosm. I am the macrocosm.

The Sixth Attention was the birth of the insight that true significance does not sit in the outward; it sits in the inward. It was, however, a discovery in metaphor. I discovered that for me, things do not exist independently of my definition of them. In the Eighth Attention, the significance and superordina- cy of the inward ceases to be metaphorical; it becomes a lived, tactile experience. When such a person looks at the furthest horizon, he finds himself there.

The Eighth Attention is the only Attention that admits of no imbalance. It is perfectly poised between the binary opposites of form and meaning. In Sufism, this would be described as the goblet having become the wine. Because there is no longer the pretense of existing as an object, there is no difference between what goes on in the inward and the manifested. They are the same.

THE EIGHT ATTENTIONS

INSIGNIFICANCE	FORM	OUTWARD	SEPARATION	SIGNIFICANCE	MEANING	INWARD	GATHEREDNESS
1	2 From Inward to Outward	3 From Gatheredness to Separation	4 From Insignificant to Significant	5 From Form to Meaning	6 From Outward to Inward	7 From Separation to Gatheredness	8 Form and Meaning are the same

1st Intent	2nd Intent	3rd Intent	4th Intent
I AM HERE TO GET	*I GIVE TO GET*	*I GET TO GIVE*	*I AM HERE TO GIVE*
Infant	Adolescent	Adult	Mature

THE FOUR INTENTS

⇧ ⇧ ⇧ ⇧ ⇧ ⇧ ⇧ ⇧

BIRTH — **DEATH**

TAKE — **GIVE**

Encompass

The horns of my seeing
extend from the corners of my eyes to embrace the furthest horizon.
I am the young bull,
I rock the heavens with my gait as I walk the hills
I embrace it all, keeping it close
like an infant to my milky breast.

It is all mine,
I hold it all in my encompass,
the lantern moon hanging from the vault,
the awakening of the sun,
its stretching bright and setting sleep,
all are stretched round by the bubble tent called me
enclosing the emptiness within which
the four corners of the wind roar from me to me
through the firmament, the clarity
where once there was my head.

Chapter 7

THE PRACTICE OF CLARIFYING ATTENTION
Silencing Internal Dialogue

W here the key to clarifying intent is to shift the register of internal dialogue from resentment to gratitude; the key to clarifying attention is the silencing of internal dialogue. These two skills enable each other. On the one hand, the more a person's intent is based on appreciation and gratitude, the less stormy their internal realm becomes. On the other hand, the quieter a person is within, the easier it is for them to see things as they are – and therefore appreciate them.

When a person's intent is here to get, their attention becomes outwardly gathered, meaning that the other has power over the inner condition of the self. If I want something from you, your ability to withhold what I want, gives you power over me. You have hooked me like a fish and my attention is pulled right up to the window of perception.

The degree to which I forgo the outcome I am trying to manage, is the degree to which the other loses their power over me. I become inwardly gathered, meaning that I operate from a deeper place within myself. The world has less hold over me, there is a greater reflective gap between what happens to me and what I do; and my inner realm is quieter and less able to be disturbed.

I am also more aware of what is going on inside me. I operate from a place within that is increasingly deep, which means that not only do I perceive the objects of the outer world, but I am increasingly able to see what is going on within me. There are fewer chances that I'll get ambushed by the whisperings that carry on in the depths of my being. Metaphorically, because I am quieter within, the inner whisperings that I barely noticed before, now become quite audible.

Predatory and Receptive Attention

We humans operate in two modes of attention, namely predatory and receptive. The difference between the two becomes apparent when you consider the difference between the following two statements:

'He is looking at me.'

or

'He is listening to me.'

If you reflect on how you feel about either of the two statements, it is immediately apparent that the first, 'he is looking at me,' produces a vague sense of disquiet and the second, 'he is listening to me,' feels more inviting. It is useful to consider the difference between the two statements from the point of view of who invades whom. When he looks at me, it is as if he is boring into me. In my disreputable youth, the precursor to a bar fight was inevitably, 'What are you looking at?'

However, when he is listening to me, he allows me into him. I feel he is not trying to dominate me; he is allowing me to appear. When he is looking at me, he challenges me for space, and we contend. When he is listening to me, he vacates space and allows me to be.

When I am needy and outwardly gathered, one could describe my attention as convex. It is as if I am pushing against the window of perception to reach out into the world to get what I want. When I am inwardly gathered, one can describe my attention as concave. Rather than my attention anxiously pushing against the window of perception, it forms an inner vessel that receives the world. When my attention is convex, it is predatory. When in is concave, it is receptive.

Predatory attention looks out at the world in judgement. Because it is driven by conditional motive, it is constantly assessing the world against the conditions that it requires. This creates an inner climate of disapproval, rendering an ongoing comment that seeks to negate things as they are, in preference to how they should be.

Receptive attention looks on the world with curiosity. Because it has forgone the outcomes it is trying to manage, it is not concerned with the world not conforming to its requirements. Rather than wanting things to be as they should be, receptive attention takes delight in things as they are.

Finally, predatory attention is fundamentally concerned with outcomes, whereas receptive attention is concerned with process. You will remember the difference between the Joe and the Fred interactions.

	MEANS	ENDS	INTENT
JOE	PERSON	JOB	TAKE
FRED	JOB	PERSON	GIVE
	PERSON?	RESULT/JOB?	

When we examined the difference between the two, it was apparent that in the Joe interaction, I was using Joe as my means to achieve a result, and in the Fred case, I was using the result or the job as my means to enable him.

If one considers the difference between the two interactions from the point of view of my attention, it will be clear that in the Joe interaction my attention is fundamentally aimed at the outcome, something outside of the moment. In the Fred interaction my attention is on him, in the moment.

This suggests that I can conduct any activity consistently with the shift of attention described in these two interactions. I can walk up a mountain using my attention consistently with the Joe interaction, or I can do so consistently with the Fred interaction. If I walk up the mountain consistently with the Joe interaction, I will say to you I am walking to get to the top of the mountain. The aim of the process of walking is to achieve an outcome, the top of the mountain. If I am walking up the mountain using my attention consistently with the Fred interaction, I will say the top of the mountain is my means to walk well. The purpose of the walking is to walk, and the top of the mountain is my means to achieve that purpose.

Silencing Internal Dialogue

Silencing internal dialogue through meditation is the core practice for clarifying attention. It is based on the premise that what disables one's ability to see things as they are, is the degree to which there is an inner clamour. It may appear that first you have to become quiet, and then you can start seeing things as they are. This approach to the problem is really challenging and will be the source of many hours of frustration. However, try the following:

Preparatory Exercise 1:

1. Look around the room you are in and identify any colour. Once you have done this, look around the rest of the room and deliberately identify all other objects that have the same colour. Once you have done this, repeat the exercise with two more colours.

2. Close your eyes and try to identify the furthest sound you can hear and rest your attention on it for a while. Repeat the exercise with a sound in the middle distance and, after resting your attention on that for a while, repeat the exercise with the closest sound you can hear.

Now consider how much internal chatter is going on and you will probably find that you were significantly quieter after you did the exercise than before doing it. The truth of the matter is an inversion from what we described above. If you want to become quiet, then rest your attention on something that is actually taking place in the moment you are in.

Internal dialogue leaches attention. All the words, images and impressions that play on the inner screen of the mind leach away the sum of attention that is available in any given moment. When you deliberately rest your attention on something that is actually going on, you are summoning attention away from this inner screen and your inner realm becomes quieter. This implies that rather than silencing internal dialogue to see things as they are, see things as they are and the internal dialogue will quieten.

What is very important here, though, is that you must restrict your attention to physical experiences. I don't think it is helpful to 'focus' on any sensations. Also, the description of the practice as 'resting' your attention on something is quite deliberate.

Bearing the difference between predatory and receptive attention in mind, clearly the idea of focussing is very visual and invokes predatory attention.

Whilst predatory attention judges, receptive attention savours. So, the mode of attention you need to exercise here is very much like listening. It is about resting your attention on the sensation that you are giving attention to in a gentle and savouring way, rather than focussing.

Preparatory Exercise 2:

1. Find a pleasant place outside where you can sit for between half an hour and an hour.
2. Deliberately cycle between your senses, one at a time. When you are listening, only listen. When you are looking, give full attention to the image. When you are feeling, close your eyes and rest your attention on the tactile sensations of the wind and warmth of the sun playing on your skin. If you can, smell and taste as well.
3. When you are finished, consider the following:
    1. Are you more or less noisy on the inside after having done this?
    2. How do you feel emotionally?
    3. Was there a difference between which senses you used and how quiet you became?

Considering what we discussed regarding the difference be- tween predatory and receptive attention, it is not surprising that when people are looking, they are generally noisier on the inside. This is because our eyes are the most predatory of our five senses.

All our other senses fundamentally have a receptive char- acter. After this exercise you are likely to feel quieter inside. You are also likely to feel more relaxed, calm and rested. Quite possibly you may also feel happier.

The previous two exercises are designed to give you an experience of what a meditative state feels like. Having dis- covered this, what we will now explore is the basic practice of silencing internal dialogue – which should be done on a daily basis.

This practice should be done at least once a day, for twenty minutes to half an hour at a time.

Core Meditation Practice:

1. Sit comfortably with your back relaxed but erect.

2. Look around the room you are in and identify any colour. Once you have done this, look around the rest of the room and deliberately identify all other objects that have the same colour. Now repeat the exercise with two more colours.

3. Close your eyes and try to identify the furthest sound you can hear and rest your attention on it for a while. Repeat the exercise with a sound in the middle distance and, after resting your attention on that for a while, repeat the exercise with the closest sound you can hear.

4. Bring your attention into your body and feel your body from the inside, top to bottom. Should you notice any tension in this process, deliberately let go of the tension.

5. Settle your attention on your breath. Feel your breath come in and go out.

6. If you notice that your attention has wandered, gently bring it back to your breath.

7. At the end of the meditation it is important to take a few minutes to emerge from the state. Don't immediately jump up and rush off.

It is very likely that the first few attempts at meditating will be somewhat frustrating. Having shown many people how to do this over the years, the following are some of the typical concerns people voice:

'I feel I am wasting my time. I think I am more noisy inside when I meditate.'

It is very unlikely that meditation will make you noisier inside. What is more likely to happen, is that you become aware of the level of the noise which is already there. Most of

our attention is so outwardly gathered that we are unaware of the noise that is going on inside.

'My first few meditations were very good, but now I can't seem to get any depth.'

The conditioning that has the most profoundly debilitating effect on us is subtle and is kept in place by a whispered internal dialogue of which we are not aware.

At some point, our meditation will cause this quiet whispering to surface, and if its effect on us has been profound, it is likely to surface with a roar. The experience of this is that your meditation becomes very agitated, so much so that it may seem that you have lost the skill and that you are wast ing your time.

Don't despair! There is no such thing as a wasted meditation. Sometimes the noisiest ones are the ones that have the most cathartic effect.

'I suffer terrible headaches from meditating.'

Provided that you are following the caution to use receptive attention rather than focus, it is unlikely that your meditation will cause a headache. What is far more likely is that the headache is a cathartic experience and is concerned with something clarifying or being released. Stay with the practice. It will get easier in time. Other discomforts may surface, such as tension in the shoulders or in the jaw. The same insight holds true.

'I keep on falling asleep.'

Because we live in a very sleep-deprived culture, many people are deeply exhausted. This exhaustion surfaces when

you meditate and should not be resisted. If you need to sleep, then sleep.

'I am uncomfortable meditating sitting up. Can I lie down?'

The mode of attention we are trying to cultivate here is relaxed alertness. Meditating lying down is possible, but it is very likely that you will fall asleep. It is better to develop the skill of being able to do this sitting up.

The Use of Affirmations

The use of affirmations is a very powerful way of boosting your meditation, although it does require you to have some basic skill. It is therefore advisable only to start working with affirmations after having developed some proficiency with your meditation. An affirmation is a phrase or a word referring to something that you seek to cultivate. This affirmation is repeated while you meditate.

The technique is to rest your attention on your breath for two breaths and on the third breath to shift your attention to the affirmation. It is useful not to think of the affirmation as a loud and explicit thought. Allow it to be whimsical, almost as if you can hear it on your breath. You then shift the atten- tion back to the breath for two breaths and on the third, you shift your attention to the affirmation once again.

Affirmations do come with a health warning: The general rule is that they should seek to cultivate a state in the self and not a transformation in the world. It is, for example, quite contrary to what we are proposing here to repeat some- thing to the effect of 'I will win a million'.

Any given affirmation should be repeated at least three times and you really should not be working with more than seven affirmations at a time.

The following is a useful set of affirmations based on the transactional correctness model:

- I see things as they are.
- The world is my benefactor.
- I am deeply grateful.
- The world is my ally.
- I trust the future.
- I submit.
- I am in awe.

Attention to Process over Outcome and Flow

The celebrated psychologist Mihaly Csikszentmihalyi has coined the term flow, which refers to the experience that people have when what they do is inherently satisfying. In essence, Csikszentmihalyi argues that anything done with true autotelic (having an end or purpose in itself) intent can become transformatively fulfilling.

What Csikszentmihalyi is calling on, is a shift of attention from outcome to process. It is the attention of a person who uses the top of the mountain to walk well, rather than walk- ing to get to the top of the mountain. His ground-breaking insight here is that this use of attention can be applied to any activity, which means that any activity can become the means whereby one cultivates attention.

His work brings to mind a quote from "A Day in the Life of Ivan Denisovich" by Alexandr Solzhenitsyn:

Shukov found a place for the seat of his wadded trousers. .... When he did so his coat and jacket tightened, and he found something sharp press- ing against the left side of his chest.... It was the edge of the hunk of bread in his little inner pocket- that half ration which he had taken with him for dinner......

He laid his mittens on his knees, unbuttoned his coat, untied the tapes of his face-cloth, stiff with cold, folded it several times over and put it away in his knee pocket. Then he reached for the hunk of bread, wrapped in a piece of clean cloth, and, holding the cloth at chest level so that not a crumb should fall to the ground, began to nibble and chew at the bread. The bread, which he had carried under two garments, had been warmed by his body. The frost hadn't caught it at all.

More than once during his life in the camps, Shu- kov had recalled the way they used to eat in his village: whole saucepans of potatoes, pots of por- ridge and, in the early days, chunks of meat. And milk to split their guts. That wasn't the way to eat, he learned in camp. You had to eat with all your mind on the food – like now, nibbling the bread bit by bit, working the crumbs up into a paste with your tongue and sucking it into your cheeks. And how good it tasted, that soggy black bread.

The implication of Csikszentmihalyi's work is that one can do any activity consistently with how Solzhenitsyn describes Shukov's eating; from playing an instrument, to climbing rocks, to performing surgery and brushing your teeth – they can all be activities that cultivate attention.

The essence of the approach is to deliberately shift your attention from outcome into process. To make the point of what you are doing to do it well and to use the outcome you are trying to pursue as an opportunity to commit to doing the activity as well as you can. This can clearly be adopted as a methodology for daily life, to consistently give full atten- tion to what you are doing and to take the time to do it well, rather than just to rush through the experience.

Walking Meditation

There is a Buddhist practice of walking meditation that resonates deeply with what Csikszentmihalyi describes. It amounts to walking very slowly, giving full attention to all the small movements of the body and being very deliberate with regard to what you are doing in every moment: The lift ing of your foot, the shifting of your weight, the putting down of your foot, the transfer of your balance to the other side and the moving of your other foot.

Walking Meditation for Receptive Attention

The following practice is based on the insight that while our eyes are used in a principally predatory way and all our other senses are fundamentally receptive, we can use any of these senses to either of these purposes. This means that one can also use one's vision in a receptive way. In order to understand how to do this, you first have to distinguish between attention and focus.

One clearly can give attention to something you are not focussed on. If you focus on something immediately ahead of you, it is also possible to notice something in your peripheral vision and give attention to what is in your peripheral vision by shifting your focus. When one gives attention to what sits in your peripheral vision, there are a number of effects.

The first effect is that you experience the world that comes to you rather than the world you want to go to. This is best explained by way of metaphor. A lion has eyes like ours because it too is a predator. Its eyes are binocular and are placed in the front of its head to enable depth perception and focus. This depth perception allows it to judge distance and see what it needs to do to achieve the outcome of bringing down its prey. Our capacity to perceive depth and our capacity to visualise into the future are deeply related skills. By contrast, the eyes of an antelope sit on the sides of itshead. Its vision is not built around what it wants to get, but rather what wants to get it. In this sense, its vision is receptive rather than predatory.

The second effect of giving attention to what sits in your peripheral vision is that you inhabit a world of movement rather than a world of objects. When you focus on some- thing, you make it crisp, you identify its outlines so that it becomes solid. It becomes a still object in the middle of your field of vision. Should you keep on focussing on a train moving through a landscape, for example, the train would stand still in the middle of your field of vision and the landscape would move around the train. We apprehend movement in our peripheral vision and we make things inert when we fo cus on them. Receptive attention produces an experience of the world as energy and flow; predatory attention produces a world of solidity and denseness.

The third effect of receptive attention is that you experience outcomes to come to you rather than you having to go to them. Imagine that you are walking down a straight road of two kilometres with tall trees at the end and trees lining either side of the road. Imagine that you focus on the trees at the end and walk with the intention to get there.

The effect on your attention is that you would be outwardly gathered; you would probably be leaning slightly for- ward in the effort of pushing into the future to get there. Now imagine that you walk the same distance, but this time, while you are still focussing on the trees at the end of the road, you also give attention to the trees on either side of the road in your peripheral vision.

The effect of this will be that, rather than experiencing yourself as pushing into the future, the world is slipping past you. In a sense, you are not doing the work; the world is doing the work. Your legs are making the same movement, but there is not the same experience of strain. The world has become a treadmill and you are perfectly poised in the moment, twiddling your legs. You do not go to the outcome; the outcome comes to you.

When your intent is conditional and your attention is predatory, you experience the world as challenging. Outcomes remain far away and require a lot of energy to pursue. After all, it is the nature of the other animals to flee the lion. When your attention is receptive, you experience the world as your ally. It brings the outcomes to you and you experience that you do not expend a lot of effort for benign outcomes to happen.

You don't need to force your world because it wants to deliver for you.

The peripheral vision walking meditation is based on this insight. All you need to do it is a reasonably open piece of road where you will not have to commit too much attention to avoiding vehicles. As you walk, focus on what is in front of you, but rest your attention on your peripheral vision, on the world as it slips past you. You will notice a very peculiar pleasure when you walk this way. You will also find a dramatic decrease in the volume of your internal dialogue.

ABOUT THE AUTHOR

E tsko Schuitema is the founder of the Schuitema Group, a consultancy dedicated to the enhancement of human excellence based on the Care & Growth™ model.

Born into a mining family in South Africa, Etsko grew up in Johannesburg. After doing an Honours degree in Social Anthropology at the University of the Witwatersrand, he got a job as a graduate researcher with The Chamber of Mines of South Africa's Research Organisation.

Employed specifically by the Human Resources Laboratory of the organisation, his work initially focused on the issue of conflict on gold mines in South Africa. At the end of the overthrow of the apartheid regime, the mines were swept up in the upheaval that followed. The work he did led to the development of a framework for understanding trust in this very volatile environment.

Using this basis of this research he was asked to head the Human Resources Laboratory's Industry Project and implement his insights. This is where Care & Growth™ model originated. It was met with significant success within the mining sector. Such success in fact that Etsko left his role with the Chamber of Mines and along with a group of colleagues, to establish a consultancy where this model could be more widely disseminated.

Over the past 30 years, The Schuitema Group under the leadership of Etsko has, alongside several associates, worked in over 26 countries in a large range of sectors, creating powerful working relationships to implement the Care & Growth™ model empowering individuals on all levels of these organisations.

Etsko Schuitema is a renowned business consultant who has authored numerous books including 'Leadership' and 'The Millenium Discourses'. He is a senior partner in Schuitema, a transformational consultancy operating worldwide. Etsko is also a Shaykh or teacher in the Shadhili-Darqawi Sufi tradition and is known as Shaykh Ebrahim.□

Other Books by Etsko Schuitema